Who's
in charge
Anyway?

Who's
in charge
Anyway?

How Parents Can Teach Children
to Do the Right Thing

KATHY LYNN

foreword by **BARBARA COLOROSO**

whitecap

Edited by Holly Bennett
Proofread by Lesley Cameron
Cover design by Roberta Batchelor
Comic strips © Lynn Johnston Productions, Inc. Reproduced by permission.
Interior design by Margaret Lee / bamboosilk.com

Printed and bound in Canada

National Library of Canada Cataloguing in Publication Data

Lynn, Kathy, 1946-
   Who's in charge anyway? : how parents can teach children to do the right thing /
Kathy Lynn ; foreword, Barbara Coloroso.

   Includes index.
   ISBN 1-55285-469-8

   1. Parenting. 2. Moral education. I. Title.
HQ769.L96 2003   649'.7   C2003-910803-1

The publisher acknowledges the support of the Canada Council and the Cultural
Services Branch of the Government of British Columbia in making this publication
possible. We acknowledge the financial support of the Government of Canada through
the Book Publishing Industry Development Program for our publishing activities.

Thanks to Alia, Andrew, Bill, Bobbie, Cynthia, Elija, Haley, Heather, Josh, Katie,
Madelene, Paula, Samantha, Sheila, Soraya, Tanya, and Virginie for providing the
interior photos.

To the women who have been my mentors and guides:

NANO MCCONNELL, *my teacher and friend*
She led me to the start of this parenting education path and has encouraged me all along.

EDNA NASH, *the grandmother of parenting education*
Her calls to me when I slipped off the rails helped me maintain my focus on the task of parenting education and stay true to the beliefs we share.

EVELYN DONLEVY
She simply accepted me and believed in me.

CONTENTS

ACKNOWLEDGEMENTS

THIS BOOK WOULD NOT EXIST WITHOUT THE HELP AND SUPPORT of many people. My sincere thanks go to:

The folks from Whitecap Books: Robert McCullough and Leanne McDonald who trusted me with this project; Robin Rivers who shepherded me through the editing process; and Sophie Hunter who helped the world find out the book exists.

My editor Holly Bennett, who made certain that my writing was clear and was exactly what I really wanted to say. It is as much her book as mine.

Barbara Coloroso, who took time from her busy schedule to write the foreword and who has always been available with encouragement and advice.

My colleagues, the parenting educators who work to help parents with this tough job of child-raising. A special thanks to Fran Kammermayer who encouraged me throughout the process.

Julie Ferguson of Beacon Literary Services and Maria Holman of the law firm Beechinor Baker Hall who handled the business side of this endeavour.

My parents Tom and Chris Foley, who demonstrated quality parenting as they raised me.

My husband John and children Chelsea and Foley, who permitted me to tell their stories in print.

The thousands of parents who honor me with their presence at my presentations each year and who call me on my radio program with their questions and comments. It is for their children that this book exists.

THROUGHOUT MY PROFESSIONAL CAREER I HAVE ARGUED THAT there is no recipe for parenting. There is no tried and true collection of techniques for raising children and there are no experts who can give parents the secrets of success. There are, however, ideas and approaches that can be explored. There are ways to foster self-esteem and opportunities to teach children to act with integrity, civility and compassion; there are tools that can help teach children the principles of mutual respect and personal responsibility. We as parents have tremendous power to set the standards for acceptable behavior and to model and teach those standards. Using this power wisely is key to helping our children develop the ability to do what is right, rather than what is merely easy; to help our children develop the habits of justice, honesty, fairness and sharing.

These habits require that children develop an inner moral voice or personal code that guides them to do or say what is decent, caring and compassionate, in spite of external consequences and never merely because of them. By developing such a voice, children can discover the kind of persons they are trying to be. Kids need to know we care as much about their intent as we do about their actions. We must teach them to reflect on the impact of their actions on other people and be able to see things from another's point of view. By taking on another's perspective and feeling empathy toward that person, when faced with difficult situations, kids are more likely to know what is the right thing to do. Kids develop this inner voice by emulating the important adults in their lives.

Who's in Charge Anyway? is a book that gives parents practical, useful and thoughtful advice on how to be the parent that your child needs by using the everyday situations every family faces, such as temper tantrums, bedtime, whining, dawdling, sibling rivalry, chores, money matters, table manners and teens baulking at curfew. A respected parenting educator for over twenty-five years, Kathy Lynn demonstrates practical ways to help kids grow into mature, responsible adults, by giving them the opportunity to make their own decisions (within safe, moral limits) and bear responsibility for the outcome.

Filled with stories every parent can relate to, and brimming with a perfect blend of philosophical practicality, Kathy's book explains:
• The importance of *your* values and behavior
• The difference between discipline and punishment
• How to get kids motivated to mind, not made to mind
• The pitfalls of too much praise
• That your teens still need you
• Creating a balance with your kids' activities
and much more.

Above all, *Who's in Charge Anyway?* is a book that gives parents practical, useful and thoughtful advice to help their children grow into responsible, resourceful and resilient people who treat themselves and others with dignity and regard.

BARBARA COLOROSO
Educator and author of *kids are worth it! Giving Your Child the Gift of Inner Discipline, Parenting Through Crisis* and *The Bully, The Bullied and the Bystander.*

INTRODUCTION

PARENTING EDUCATION IS MY PASSION. CHILDREN ARE MY CLIENTS and parents and professionals are my audiences. Twenty-five years ago I realized that nothing mattered as much to me as the next generation, our children. That's when I founded Parenting Today and started designing and delivering parenting education workshops.

In 1987, I began publishing a newsletter; each issue contains an educational article as well as updates on the activities of Parenting Today. People responded positively and often.

But in November 1997 I wrote a short article called "Children Need to Do the Right Thing" and the response was overwhelming. My phone rang off the hook and many of the calls were long distance. "Can we reprint your article in our newsletter?" "Parents need to hear this message." "Can you expand on the topic?"

In this book I talk about the role of parents to be the leaders, to set the standards of our children's behavior and to take charge of the parenting role. Unless we expect, model, demand and supervise those standards, our kids won't learn to do what's right, rather than what's easy.

Today's children seem to be floundering. They know about being their own person and meeting their own needs. And these are good things. But somehow, in helping our children to feel good about themselves, we've missed the boat on helping them develop character.

Dan Bortolotti, former managing editor at *Today's Parent* magazine, once wrote that a sign of character is the ability to internalize your values — to do the right thing simply because it *is* the right thing. How does that fit with today's value of allowing children to do their own thing?

It's a dilemma. Allowing our children to meet their own needs and have high self-esteem, and raising them to be of good character are both laudable parenting goals — yet they seem to be at odds with each other.

They aren't, though. The irony is that children who are asked to do their best and be their best, and are permitted to work through the consequences of their decisions (both positive and negative), are *more* likely to be the children who grow up with high self-esteem. High self-esteem comes from effort and success, not from getting away with everything and anything. And children who learn to assess the probable results before making a choice end up making wiser choices and being automatically more successful.

It's easier said than done because the community, while saying they want children to be of good character, aren't offering many positive role models for parents or children. Everywhere we look we see examples of people doing their own thing instead of doing the right thing. We cut each other off in traffic and ignore our lunch companion to answer the cell phone. When a good citizen finds another person's lost property and returns it, it's not an expected behavior; it's news. But it doesn't have to be that way. We can reverse the trend — one parent at a time and one family at a time.

Our job as parents is to do what we need to do to raise our children to be the best citizens they can be. When my children were younger and I reacted in an inappropriate manner, my daughter would say to me: "Mom, what would you say to a parent in one of your groups?" She clearly wanted me to take charge and to be fair. I hope this book helps you to do the same.

Chapter 1

SETTING THE STAGE
VALUES CLARIFICATION

THE FOG ROLLED IN, ENVELOPING US IN A MAGICAL WORLD.
My husband John and I were camping on the beach on the west
coast of Vancouver Island. Each afternoon the fog would arrive
and we would sit in this gray world, listening to the waves we
could not see lap on the shore.

And we talked. I was five months pregnant with our first
child and we were looking forward to the birth of this baby with
excitement and nervousness. Our conversation was about this new
adventure in our lives. We didn't talk about nursery furniture or
diapers. We talked about our goals and wishes. What did we want
for this child when she was 18?

We talked about our childhoods in ways we hadn't before.
What had our parents done with us that we liked? What were our
favorite memories? Story followed story. Memories of Christmases,

birthdays, family dinners, summer trips and playing in the lane behind the house (him) and in the bush behind the house (me). Sitting in front of our tent in this private, mystical world created by the fog, we made promises to each other and to ourselves about how we wanted to raise our children.

In retrospect, this was probably the most important parenting job we did. It set the scene for the next 20 years as we raised our daughter and then our son. In the hurly-burly of child-raising, the task of setting goals can get lost. The total focus becomes diapers and sleep deprivation, playing at the park, getting ready for school and soccer practice. The doing of child-raising takes over and fills our days. It can be hard to see beyond the next bedtime, let alone the next 20 years.

But goal-setting makes it so much easier to make decisions as you go along on this child-raising road. How, you can ask yourself, will this decision, consequence, conversation, help your child reach the goals you've set?

For example, you've decided you want your child to be able to problem-solve and make decisions when she's 18. But here you are constantly telling her what to do, solving all her problems, saving her from all her mistakes. Whoops! The only way she will reach the goal of being a problem-solver is to have the opportunity to practice while she's maturing.

VALUES AND LIFESTYLE

As a couple you've made certain lifestyle choices, probably without even really thinking about it. Now it's time to take a hard look at the way you live. Having a child brings into focus every aspect of your life.

Lifestyle goes far beyond your recreational activities. It includes the choices you make during your day. Part of the discussion about your goals for your child will be determined by your values and beliefs. If someone were to ask me about my values I could probably come up with a few obvious choices, like respect and honesty. But when I get into a conversation about how I live and the choices I make, then I start to understand more about my values. When I make a lifestyle choice simply and comfortably, you can be certain that it fits with my personal values. When I make a choice just because it seems quick and easy, I'm not comfortable because the choice isn't congruent with my beliefs. How I choose to live is informed and influenced by my beliefs.

Once you are a parent this becomes more important, because it influences your child as she watches to see if how you live fits with what you say. You will find that you will also feel more strongly about some of your choices.

For example, maybe you were raised as a church-going member of a religion but lately you've been just too busy. You haven't been to church in quite some time and it hasn't really mattered. But now, there's going to be a child. Do you want her to go to church? Which church? Are you going to send her off to Sunday school while you lounge in bed or are you going to attend with her? What if you and your partner were raised in different religions?

As two childless adults, each able to make your own choices and able to change your minds at will, you've been able to simply live from day to day without really agonizing about your lifestyle. As parents you're going to find each lifestyle decision fraught with meaning. A classic example is language. Kids learn

---

Some Values/Lifestyle Questions

These are some of the questions that may come up as you create your own family lifestyle.

RELIGION: How were you raised and how do you want to raise your child?

MEALTIME: Formal or unstructured? What about fast food? Is daily dessert necessary? Table manners? Saying Grace?

CELEBRATIONS: Are birthdays important? Which holidays will you celebrate?

FAMILY: How much do you want to include your extended family in your life?

EDUCATION: Is education important to you? Do you want to have lots of books around for your child? What about university?

TOYS: What sort of toys? Will you let her play with guns? Can your son play with dolls? What about messy or noisy toys?

to speak by listening and imitating. One day your sweet innocent little muffin may stamp her tiny feet and with real intensity say, "Goddamn it!" Whoops, where did she learn that? Look in the mirror and you'll find out.

Take stock of the way you live and ask yourselves, is this how we want to raise our child? Talking about it ahead of time makes life so much simpler and avoids all kinds of emotional arguments.

As John and I sat in the fog we talked about what was important to each of us. We discovered that we weren't going to have our kids raised in the church, but we would make sure they had a sense of ethics and values and belief in a greater good. We decided that family dinners mattered. We'd sit at a properly set table, the TV would be off, there would be cloth not paper napkins and we'd have conversations. Mind you, we did miss the part about who irons the cloth napkins!

GOALS

Raising kids can be a minute-to-minute challenge. They grow and change so quickly, they move so fast. You're busy just trying to keep up. At the end of the day have your decisions made any sense? Do they fit into any pattern or are they the result of simple panic as you try to maintain some sort of order?

Setting goals and thinking long-term may seem a silly waste of time. After all, you have no idea what kind of child you're going to have. It's true that you will have to adapt your parenting approach to your child's individual needs. But you can set generic goals. What do you want for your child when she's 18?

Do you want her to be ready for a job or post-secondary education? Do you want her to be independent or obedient? Do you hope she'll be a rebel or a conformist?

When you set long-term goals, no matter how general, it will make your parenting easier and more congruent no matter how chaotic life becomes. When she's throwing a tantrum at the mall, in the back of your mind, rather than simply wondering how you can end this and end it now, you can think: "Is what I'm about to do now going to help her become that 18-year-old I've imagined?" It becomes second nature and gives real stability to your parenting decisions. As John and I talked together, we learned that we wanted our child to be independent, a good problem-solver and her own person.

HOW DOES THIS HELP — REALLY?

If you're reading this book while you're pregnant you have an advantage. It's easier to take the time for these conversations before you have kids. But no matter what the age of your children, go for it.

Without a clear understanding of your goals, beliefs and wishes for your child, your parenting decisions will be reactive. When you need to deal with a problem, you'll simply go with your mood of the moment or whatever it takes to create peace and harmony. But having a long-term goal gives you that constant focus. Your decisions will look to the future and how today's action can impact tomorrow.

Once your child reaches adolescence she's going to test all your beliefs and values and if you're not clear on what they are, parenting a teen can be the most frustrating task imaginable. But when you've been consistent throughout her life, she may still test — but both you and she will know the ultimate answer and decision.

Children need good leadership from their parents. That is more important today than ever before because the traditional community models provided by the church, school and neighborhood are incongruent. It's about setting the standards for our children's behavior and teaching them how to do the right thing. To do this, you have to know what *is* the right thing! What do you want them to learn? Then model it, teach it and expect it.

HOW DO WE TEACH VALUES?

Children learn the values we want them to embrace by observing our behavior. They watch how we live, what we do and how we treat other people. When we are honest and treat people well they see that. Values are absorbed, not taught.

Jill's mom took Jill and three of her friends to the zoo. They were there to celebrate Jill's fifth birthday. The birthday was in two days, so she was still four but one of her friends was already five.

The sign at the gate said that children under five were admitted for free. Mom told the ticket taker that one of the kids was already five and the other three were four. And the kids learned about honesty. All the lectures in the world about telling the truth are not as valuable as how we live and the choices we make.

We also model, and teach, our children to follow the social conventions we think are important. Children need to understand the expectations of their culture. But remember that conventions are not the same as our core, ethical values. Trustworthiness never goes out of style. White gloves in church may!

When I was eleven I learned a lesson about doing the right thing. My father parked the car in front of the home of a family friend. He looked at his watch, and then pulled back into the traffic.

"Isn't that where we're going for dinner?" I asked.

"Yes."

"Weren't we invited for six o'clock?"

"Yes."

"Well, my watch says six so why are we leaving?"

"While it's important to be prompt," my father explained, "when you're invited to a home for dinner you should always give your hosts an extra five minutes to be prepared." We drove around the block, reparked and went up to the door. My father pushed the doorbell at 6:05 p.m. precisely.

Ten years later, I had started to entertain on my own and discovered that not everyone had learned the same lesson. For some people, the invitation time is only a suggestion!

Though social conventions may change, my father's lesson of consideration for one's host is still relevant. What mattered to me was that he had a reason for his behavior and I learned to think about the effect my actions had on others.

IN OTHER WORDS...

Setting goals for our child-raising challenges is the easiest way to stay on track as we struggle with the day-to-day realities of parenting children.

The clearer you are about your values and beliefs, the easier it will be to set your goals. So talk to each other, set goals and get on with the task of raising strong, independent and self-disciplined children.

Talking about Behavior
Kathy's Q & A

QUESTION

I'm having trouble maintaining a balance between family time, church, school, sports, piano, violin, and on and on. We have two boys, ages five and ten. Our life seems so busy that I feel I don't have any control and my head feels like it is spinning most of the time. My children are often cranky and quarreling and I am yelling and miserable more often than I can even tolerate. This is not what I thought it would be like. I am not happy with myself.

When I try to slow things down and have a relaxing day, it seems my boys just start arguing and then I wondered why we stayed home — I might as well have them enrolled in something. My five-year-old leaves kindergarten each day asking if he can have someone over. His social life is exhausting. My ten-year-old has 5:30 a.m. hockey practices. It takes two days for us to recover and I find I resent them.

When I do have a break from work there is endless housekeeping to do. It would be nice to have an outing to the library or something quiet but there seems to be no time. On top of it all I try to help out at school and at church. I end up awake at two in the morning, not looking forward to how tired I will be the next day.

ANSWER

You need a vacation.

Not a cruise or trip to Mexico. Take a vacation from the merry-go-round of your current life. Slow things down.

Start by letting the kids each choose one extra-curricular activity and let the rest go for now. Taking a break from sports or music will not hurt the kids.

Then you need to make a choice for you. You don't need to help out everywhere right now. Some things can wait.

Next, involve the whole family in the housework. Start by holding weekly family meetings to discuss the schedule and chores. List all the jobs that need to be done and ask each of them to choose two. You will have to show them how to do the work, but then relax and let them do it to the best of their ability.

It's going to take some time for the kids to learn to slow down. They've been so busy, they just don't know how to handle a relaxing time. Be patient, break out the board games, get a supply of library books and provide art and craft supplies. You'll soon find out what they like to do and they'll learn to slow down.

For more on family meetings see Chapter 12: Putting It All Together.

QUESTION

My ten-year-old wants me to take him to adult movies. I don't think he should be seeing that amount of violence but he nags constantly and says that all his friends get to go to these movies. Am I being unfair?

ANSWER

From his perspective, yes. But then ten-year-olds often charge their parents with being unfair.

Parents have a responsibility to demonstrate the values they want their children to emulate and children will push at the limits. This is typical and healthy.

"All my friends get to go," is the most common complaint of preteens and teens. Although you're tempted to respond with, "If all your friends were going to jump off a bridge would you follow them?" this sort of sarcasm will get you nowhere.

Your job is to decide which movies are appropriate for your child and stick to your decision. Explain your reasons to your son, listen to his side of the issue, and respond to that. Really listen to him and be open to the possibility that he may come up with a persuasive reason to see a particular film. Then make your decision and get on with your life. He will only nag if the nagging continues to get your attention. If your only response is a boring "You know my decision on that," he will eventually stop nagging, as it'll be a waste of time.

It's also helpful to speak with his friends' parents. They are probably under the same pressure. The best situation occurs when the parents can all agree on some guidelines for movie and television viewing. Then you will know what "all the other kids" are allowed to watch.

QUESTION

My wife and I both work outside the home. I pick up my two-year-old son and eight-year-old daughter on my way home from work. My wife works later and gets home between 6:15 p.m. and 6:45 p.m. I believe that family meals are important but the children simply can't last until their mother gets home.

Any advice?

ANSWER

Hungry, tired and cranky children at the dinner table don't make for a positive family experience for anyone. You're right, family time is important but it doesn't necessarily have to happen around the dinner table.

There are a number of options open to you. One family I know with the identical problem instituted "tea time" soon after they got home. This was a substantial meal for the children. Then later they joined their parents at the dinner table for what amounted to a bedtime snack. Family dinners can be saved for weekends and holidays when all can enjoy them. Some families have made breakfast a regular family meal and this works for them.

The trick is to stay focused on your goals of positive family time, modeling table manners and the social aspects of mealtimes, while respecting the developmental needs of your children. When you do that, coming up with a plan that works for you becomes simpler.

QUESTION

I'm a first-time father who has in-laws in the same city. I am having a hard time adjusting to how much they want to see the baby. They call every day and drop in every other day. I find it frustrating and threatening because I want to spend as much time with her as I can, since my wife and I both work.

We have tried talking to them about it, letting them know that we would like some nights with no interruptions. That has worked at times, but every other day it's the same thing. Any suggestions?

ANSWER

This is a tricky situation. Your daughter is fortunate to have grandparents who care so much. Infants change so rapidly it's understandable that they want time with her. But so do you.

Try to change the timing of the visits. What about arranging for the grandparents to spend time with her while you're at work? Drop her off on your way to work. Or have them pick her up from daycare in the afternoon. This way they would get time with her and she would be with family members part of the day.

You might also involve them in helping with some of the tasks you're finding difficult to fit in. For example, ask them to pick up groceries on the way over to visit. Then they will be able to visit but will have also put some time back in your schedule.

In other words, instead of reducing the amount of time they see your daughter, see if you can rearrange the times and circumstances to meet both your needs.

Chapter 2

RITUALS & ROUTINES
THE ROOTS OF SECURITY

EIGHT-YEAR-OLD BRANDON IS SPENDING THIS WEEKEND WITH HIS mom. His parents separated when he was three and now he alternates between their homes on weekends and spends the weekdays with his mother and sister.

He can count on this schedule and knows what to expect. On this particular Saturday afternoon, he's covered with flour because he and his mom are baking a cake. It's his birthday tomorrow and one of the family rituals is that the birthday person gets to choose what kind of cake he wants and can help bake it if he chooses. Brandon loves to cook with his mom so here he is up to his elbows in butter, chocolate and flour.

My daughter tells me about a conversation she had with her friends in her first year at university. She was away from home and looking forward to joining us for Christmas. She told her friends that the night she arrived home we would have escargots, a fondue, Caesar salad, and ice-cream sundaes for dessert. They were confused; how did she know? Had she called home and placed an order for this meal?

Actually, no, we hadn't talked about it at all. But she knew that when we have a major celebration in our home that is the menu of choice, and that she could count on the fact that her coming home would rate the celebratory dinner. And she was correct.

Rituals like these are touchstones for our children. Whether it's a daily routine such as a bedtime story followed by a snuggle or all the activities surrounding a major holiday celebration, our children learn to count on them and get a tremendous sense of security from knowing what to expect.

Some rituals bring a sense of shared fun to the family: When my children were little they learned that whenever we drove under an overpass we would all duck. In our home it was a real treat to order a take-out dinner, and to add to the treat it was the one time when we watched television while we ate. So the kids would move from the menus straight to the TV guide.

Other routines make everyday life run more smoothly: a routine last trip to the bathroom before heading out the door or the practice of having each family member bring their dishes to the kitchen at the end of the meal.

Finally, the predictability of routines gives a sense of competence and control to small children in a big world. I remember hearing the story of a new preschool teacher who came into a well-established school part way through the year and decided to switch the schedule slightly. Well, it may have been a minor change to her but the children were incensed. They knew that circle time came before snack time and that was carved in stone for these youngsters.

WHAT ABOUT CHRISTMAS?

When Chelsea, my oldest child, was a baby and I was pregnant, I read a magazine article that saved our Christmas. The author of this article wisely reminded me that the perfect Christmas memories of my childhood come from when I was older, not when I was an infant. I considered my 11-month-old daughter and my rapidly expanding waistline (her brother was born three months later), and in coordination with my husband, designed a Christmas that made sense for us that year. Chelsea loved the lights on the Christmas tree, chewed happily on the boxes containing gifts, and enjoyed the relaxed and happy atmosphere of our holiday season.

Many parents see Christmas or other major holiday celebrations as a time for children and assume they must do everything possible to make the holiday a perfect and memorable experience for their kids. But every Christmas is not perfect — nor does it have to be. Like everyone else, I sometimes get so involved in my dreams and expectations that I come close to ruining Christmas for myself and everyone around me. But there are some guidelines that can help make Christmas a good time for all family members.

Extended family

Discuss your expectations and values with all family members who may be present. Many problems arise due to a clash in values ("But we always eat at noon") or expectations ("I just assumed that if I cooked Christmas dinner, you'd have us all over for the next holiday"). Remember to deal with these issues each year there are new or different family members in town. Missing this conversation can lead to dreadfully hurt feelings that no one will understand.

Deal with whether you will be with his family or her family in a clear fashion and in a way that is fair to all.

Shopping

The obvious issue is to be in control of your budget. Purchase only things you can afford, and be realistic.

From the age of two, children should be actively involved in choosing a gift for their parents and siblings. If they have an allowance they can use it for gift purchases, or their parents can give them a certain amount of money. Having the parents buy something and putting the child's name on it is not teaching the child anything about either the joy of giving or the fun and frustration of shopping for the perfect gift within a budget. When children choose gifts themselves, they need to really think about the recipient, not themselves.

Cooking and decorating

Children love to help bake, and should be allowed to be involved. We adults often get so tied up in the need for perfection, we can't allow our children to do their best, to participate and to proudly serve the cookies or squares they baked. The kids are underfoot while you're trying to bake anyway, so you may as well get them working. These same children can take over the baking as they become 11 or 12, after a decade of marvelous training.

There are many tasks for children in the preparation of a special occasion dinner: salad preparation, washing vegetables, tearing bread for stuffing, making decorative name tags for the table, setting the table, clearing up and washing the dishes (or loading the dishwasher). All these jobs give children the opportunity of doing real work alongside adults.

Children can also participate in decorating. They love to be actively involved in choosing and decorating the tree, hanging a wreath, displaying cards and wrapping presents.

Involving our children in the Christmas celebrations helps them to build character as they learn about the work involved in making a special event happen and the great feeling that comes from having done the work to bring happiness to all family members.

IN OTHER WORDS...

The rituals and routines that we develop with our families, from the smallest quick hug in the morning to the annual trek to the family cottage, are important to our children. Children have little control over their lives and environment, so when they can count on certain activities it gives them a sense of control.

Talking about Behavior
Kathy's Q & A

QUESTION

Our four-year-old daughter is having trouble at preschool. Whenever there is a change in the routine she doesn't want to attend. Whether it's pizza day, a field trip or dress-up day she cries in the morning, saying she doesn't want to go. She's fine on regular days. How can we help her cope with this so she will see the "special days" as fun?

ANSWER

Routines and rituals are the basis for feelings of security and stability for children. Children have little control over their environment so they count on routines to provide predictability. They like to know what to expect and a change in routine can be upsetting. Some children are more flexible than others; they tend to adapt to change quite easily. Other children have difficulty with change throughout their childhood.

Your daughter needs you to understand that, for her, change isn't "fun." Listen to her fears and concerns and empathize with her difficulty in accepting the special days. Allow her to have negative feelings on those days. Simply being permitted to be unhappy may go a long way to helping her cope.

Second is to walk her through the changes ahead of time. What's going to happen? The more you can let her know about the change in routine the easier it will be for her to accept it. Help her to see the aspects of the day that will be familiar. The teacher and children will remain the same, they may be in the same place as usual and maybe you can have her wear the same outfit as yesterday.

Finally, you can let her know that sometimes things are difficult but that you have faith that she can handle it. Talk about times when you went somewhere new and how hard it was but you had fun.

She may never find it easy to accept change, but she can gain strength each time she overcomes her fear and handles a new situation.

QUESTION

My seven-year-old has started giving us a real problem at bedtime. He used to go to bed quite well but lately he complains, won't stay in bed and simply will not settle down. How can we get him to go to bed on time?

ANSWER

Children quickly learn that there are at least two things parents can't make them do. We can't make them eat and we can't make them sleep. We, on the other hand, spend a lot of our time and energy trying to accomplish both.

The first rule of bedtime is that the child must be sleepy. When a child who has normally gone to bed quite well suddenly starts fighting bedtime it's likely that he simply isn't tired. As children grow they need less sleep, so a later bedtime may be the answer.

Physical exercise improves sleep. A positive habit families can adopt is going for a walk after dinner. Walking to the park, playing for a short while and returning home benefits everyone.

You should avoid vigorous exercise, television or video games too close to bedtime. A good bedtime routine includes a snack, a quiet, warm bath and reading a story. Remember, just because your seven-year-old can read doesn't mean you should stop reading to him.

Children aren't ready for sleep at the same moment every night. You can allow a seven-year-old to control his sleep by letting him read in bed until he's ready for sleep. He must, however, stay in bed.

A relaxing routine, respecting your child's real sleep needs and spending time with him will help bedtime problems.

QUESTION

My son Adrian is in grade three this year and my daughter Caroline is starting grade one. Every year the first week of school is chaotic. I want to avoid that this year. How can I prepare them for the start of school?

ANSWER

You're wise to think ahead about the first week of school. Summer usually means a laid-back and flexible schedule. Bedtimes are later and mornings are slow and easy. Then school hits and suddenly we're trying to get the kids to bed early and up and moving in a quick and efficient fashion in the morning. And it just doesn't work well.

Two weeks before the first day of school is a good time to start. Slowly ease the children back to their regular bedtimes and start making the mornings more scheduled. Having some planned activities in the morning can really help this process. Then there's a reason to get up and moving.

Notice how much sleep they've been getting when there is no schedule. Then you can determine the amount of sleep they need and set reasonable bedtimes for the fall. Their sleep needs may have changed over the summer.

Talk to them about the expected morning routine. Get them alarm clocks and teach them how to use them. They can then take responsibility for getting up in the morning. Discuss whether they want to choose their clothes the night before, how they want to organize their school backpacks and plan who makes lunches and when. Many families find it easier to prepare lunches the night before. Giving kids the responsibility for making or helping with lunches increases the likelihood that they'll actually eat what they bring. It's also a responsibility they can handle. Adrian can probably handle the task himself and Caroline will need help.

Children need a good breakfast in order to be able to pay attention and learn. Once your kids have alarm clocks and a morning plan they can get themselves up and you can organize breakfast. For those children who simply can't face much food in the morning (more common as they get older), a cereal bar or extra piece of fruit for recess is a good idea.

While you're at it, make a plan for handling school notices. It's a good idea to have a spot designated for school notices or permission slips. If the kids can get into the habit of placing them on the counter by the phone as soon as they get home and you remember to check that spot daily, you can avoid a lot of last-minute problems.

Check out the Q&A in Chapter 13 (Child of the Community) for thoughts on kids walking to school.

QUESTION

I have an almost two-year-old son who is very attached to his blanket and thumb. He's pretty much constantly got his thumb in his mouth and, while I don't mind that he does it, he's always wet up to his elbow and can't seem to function without his blanket. I'm wondering when it would be an appropriate time to wean him off it, and how to go about doing it with the least amount of stress (for both of us!).

ANSWER

Let him have his blanket and thumb as long as he wants. He may need it for another year or two.

Children choose their own methods of stress reduction. It's best if we can simply allow them to use what they've chosen. I actually find it quite amazing that they are so good at meeting their own needs. It's also interesting to watch how different children make different choices.

Thumb-sucking can be a dental concern when it continues in an older child so you'll want to help him give that up first, but nagging or forcing him to stop won't be helpful. Watch the times when he's most likely to need his thumb and try to distract him by giving him things to hold in each of his hands. Of course, his blanket can be one of those things. His blanket isn't hurting anyone and is probably helping him. He'll give it up when he's ready.

Chapter 3

MIRROR IMAGES
MIKEY SEE, MIKEY DO

IT WAS A FOGGY MORNING AND I WAS DRIVING TO WORK.

I came up to a pedestrian-controlled intersection. The light was in my favor as I turned right. Suddenly, a woman with a four-year-old child ran across the street. In the intersection, against the light. Against the pedestrian-controlled light, through the fog.

I was reminded of the time my son and daughter, nine and ten years old, both needed glasses. Their father and I wear glasses, so this was not a surprise, and the kids enjoyed choosing their frames.

Chelsea and Foley appeared before their father, showing off their new looks. Later that evening he pointed out to me a fact that I had missed in the hurly-burly of shopping. Each child had chosen frames almost identical to those of their same-sex parent. Without being told, my children had observed and learned what style of frames is appropriate for males and females in our family.

What does this have to do with the jaywalker mother and daughter? That child, nearly old enough to be out walking and crossing streets on her own, was also learning. She was learning that it is okay to cross against a red light as long as you run.

Every school day at three p.m., many parents show up at our local elementary school to pick up their children. These parents are concerned about their children's safety. They don't want them crossing busy streets and walking home alone, so they come to the school to collect them. In school the children are told to cross streets with the crossing guard, to cross at intersections and to look both ways before crossing the street. When the parents arrive, they run across the street mid-block, ten yards up from the crossing guard, and they double-park, all too often in the crosswalk. They are all over the street. When they meet their children, they take them firmly by the hand, and jaywalk — unaware, one hopes, that they are teaching their children how to cross the street.

DO AS I SAY?

"Do as I say, not as I do" is an expression used by generations of parents. It didn't work for our parents, and it won't work for us.

We talk, we explain and we lecture. We make rules and expect compliance.

But they don't listen.

It drives us crazy. No matter how much we talk, they just aren't paying attention. Oh, but they are.

Children just don't learn much by listening. They learn by observing.

How our children act and react, their behavior, the choices they make, are not random occurrences. Their behavior is a reflection of what they see happening around them and certainly a product of careful experimentation of what works and what doesn't work.

PARENTS ARE POWERFUL ROLE MODELS

Young children will imitate and learn easily. That's the good news.

The bad news is that it's up to you to live as you wish your children to live, and behave as you wish your children to behave.

There are so many images that come to mind when I think about children imitating their parents. I see the father who lectures his child about watching too much television, as he settles into his easy chair for yet another full evening of sports or sitcoms. I see the mother who comes home after a rough day declaring, "I need a drink," then tells her daughter to handle stress by exercising.

I also see parents who hold themselves to their own values, whose children are not just *told*, but *shown* how to live with integrity.

Harold and Mary were discussing their winter vacation while loading the dishwasher. Their children Andrea, ten, and Tyler, 12, were at the kitchen table, doing their homework. "Look," Mary said. "There's a professional conference in Scottsdale in February — we could make it a combined business trip and vacation."

"Robin and James are going to that conference," remarked Harold, "and they're just going to say it's a business trip but not attend any of the events."

"I'm not comfortable with that," Mary answered, and Harold agreed. "If we're going to make this part business we'll choose a conference that is important to our work, attend it and then extend our stay in order to holiday." And the kids learned that their parents didn't let personal advantage overrule their values.

A few weeks later Andrea and Tyler went with Mary to volunteer at the food bank. And the kids learned about volunteering and giving back to the community.

WHAT LIES BENEATH

Modeling is essential, but we also need to explain things to our children so they understand what we are doing, and why. Children just accept our actions, so it's important for us to put them in a context of our values and beliefs.

Devon came home from school to find his mother busy making a huge batch of spaghetti sauce. "Oh boy, my favorite!" he exclaimed. "Looks like there's enough there for lots of dinners."

"Yes, but not for us," his mother explained. "We're going to have this for dinner tonight, but I'll freeze the extra to take to Sean's house."

Before Devon could complain, his mother went on to remind him that Sean's mother had just had a new baby and was very busy. "She needs some help from her friends right now," she said. She then asked him if he wanted to go over with her to deliver the sauce and said he could invite Devon to come back to the house to play.

When you take an elderly neighbor shopping or go visit a sick relative in the hospital, talk to your children about it. They need to understand why you do these things for other people.

SETTING PRIORITIES

Values, principles and the personal needs of family members sometimes conflict. As parents, we have to think about what's most important in any given situation.

"Yew, gross!" nine-year-old Sandy exclaimed as her father walked from the bedroom to his bathroom.

Sandy's dad, James, was confused. He sleeps naked and has never put on a robe to go for his shower. When he asked Sandy what she meant she answered, "You're disgusting, put on some clothes!"

James might have reacted to being called disgusting. He might have taken a stand on how nudity in the family is comfortable and healthy. But he didn't. Instead, he started wearing a robe when he went for his shower.

James understood that even in homes where attitudes about nudity are quite relaxed, most children will go through a modesty stage. It's important that we respect this need in our children. Happily, Sandy was able to let him know what she was feeling. Many children aren't as clear. So parents need to watch for the signals that their children are experiencing a need for privacy. Some signals are that the bathroom door is securely locked whenever they're in there, they don't want you to come in their room when they're changing, or they look away when you're not dressed. James realized that, in this case, consideration for Sandy's discomfort should take priority.

It's a question of respect for personal boundaries. By honoring our children's need for privacy, we teach them to respect themselves and others.

"I'M NOTHING LIKE YOU!"

It was the morning after the monthly parent meeting at a co-operative preschool. There was quite the hustle and bustle in the dress-up section, where a group of four-year-olds were playing. The parents who were on duty in the school that morning went over to see what was causing all the fuss.

The kids were all madly pulling on clothes as they said things like, "I have to go to the preschool meeting tonight. I do this for you, so just stay out of my way." The parents in that school had a long talk about how they behave the evening of their parent meeting. It was easy for them to make the connection between their behavior and their children's imitation.

That connection may not be so clear in the teen years. Your son comes wandering into the kitchen wearing oversized and sloppy clothing or your daughter has a tattoo on her lower back (please let it be a temporary one!). You go to look in the mirror. No, they didn't get that from you! Suddenly it seems that everything you've taught them is for naught.

Teenagers are rushing down the road to independence and self-actualization. They need to become people in their own right, not just the children of their parents. They use music, clothing and language to differentiate themselves from their parents. They are the next generation.

Wise parents understand that their teens need to make this statement. They look past the clothes and hair and see that this child still carries the basic values they have always had, and remain secure in the understanding that the strange teenage styles will pass and a young person with strong values will emerge.

THEY'RE WATCHING!

We want our kids to learn our values. We want them to develop habits of justice, honesty, fairness and sharing. But all too often we teach by talking and the kids just aren't listening.

What they are doing is watching. They watch how we live, what we do and how we treat other people.

Think about what's important to you. How did you learn it? Probably from experience and not a lecture.

So, live the way you want your kids to live.

When your children engage in behaviors or activities that bother you, ask yourself, "Where did she learn that?"

Look in the mirror and see your child.

IN OTHER WORDS...

Children learn by observation. We can talk until we're blue in the face and they may even pay attention. But when it comes to the behavior they internalize, they watch and experience much more than they listen.

Talking about Behavior
Q&A with Kathy

QUESTION

My daughter, Leanne, is in grade six. Every evening I spend one or two hours working with her on her homework. After she's in bed, I prepare all her reports on the computer. By the time she gets them to school they are perfect. And still she's not getting all A's. She needs to do well so that she can be accepted to a top university. The teacher refuses to give her the marks she needs. What more can I do?

ANSWER

Education is about learning, not about getting A's. In your effort to help Leanne be her best, you have become too involved in her learning. Homework is the task of the student, not the parent. Leanne is fortunate that you care so much but your job is to support her, not to do her homework.

The role of homework is to help the student consolidate the learning of the day, to do further study or research on a class project or to finish classroom work. She should be able to accomplish all of this on her own.

Your job is to create an environment that facilitates her learning. She needs a place to work. Some children do best in a quiet environment such as a desk in their room. Some prefer to be in the center of activity such as the kitchen table. Help her to determine when she's going to do her homework. Some children like to get it over with right after school, some need a break at that time and work much better after supper. Go with her needs.

She also needs access to resources. An encyclopedia is a good place to start. It can be an on-line version or print. If she's doing research on a particular topic you can take her to the library to pick up some books.

Be available as a resource. Let her know she can call on you if she needs help. But be careful not to take over her work. For example, if she asks the meaning of a word, send her to the dictionary rather than give her the answer. Problem-solve with her rather than give her solutions. You can say, "What do you think would happen if you did this?" In this way she'll be thinking about the material rather than just soaking up your answers.

In a more general way, you will facilitate her learning by reading to her (no, she's not too big). Encourage reading by including books as birthday gifts or subscribing to a magazine that fits her interests. An interest in and love of reading will go a long way toward her doing well in school.

Make sure she has a balance in her life. Children who also participate in physical activity usually do better in school.

Once you take the focus off marks and onto learning and once you let her do it for herself, you'll probably see an improvement. Her teacher will also thank you. She needs to see what your daughter can do on her own in order to help her do her best.

QUESTION

My three-year-old wants to wear clothing that really clashes. He'll put on green pants with a purple T-shirt and an orange sweater. What should I do?

ANSWER

Nothing. You have a child who just loves color and truly believes that the more colors he wears the more splendid he looks.

You're actually lucky that he dresses himself. And don't worry that anyone will think you chose those outfits. They'll know that your son dressed himself.

If you start criticizing his choices he'll lose his good feeling about choosing and wearing the outfits he wants to wear. It is, however, okay to have your say for special occasions.

He'll develop a better sense of style as he grows and when he's a teenager you'll remember fondly the multi-colored dresser he was when he was younger.

QUESTION

My granddaughter is five and she seems to be very hard on herself. She expects perfection in her activities, arts, crafts, sports, and even dress-up. She gets very disappointed when she does not achieve top performance on her first try.

When she tries to do something and her efforts fall short, she will withdraw and/or exhibit pouting or "crocodile tears."

Nobody in the family has high levels of achievement or expectations of perfection. Where would this come from?

We all encourage her attempts but wonder if there is something else to do. Is there a way to get her to be less critical of her efforts?

ANSWER

It could just be her personality. Some children are simply harder on themselves than others.

You can help her by letting her see you fail. When you burn dinner, let her know. "Look at that, I burned dinner. Okay, now what can I do to save the situation?"

When she's pouting or crying don't argue with her. But do problem-solve. "That was a great first try. Now what can you do next time to make it better?"

Help her determine her priorities. She is likely setting the same standards for herself for everything that she does. You can sit down with her and show her that while it's important to do her very best on a major school project, setting the table is a simple task where good enough is just fine. You also might set much smaller goals for her so she can succeed one step at a time and not get discouraged.

There is no point arguing with her, but helping her to try again will show her that she can learn from her mistakes and improve.

QUESTION

Why are toddlers so enchanted with the word "no"?

ANSWER

Children learn to speak by imitating others. They want to be grown-up like their parents, so they mimic them. And what do parents say all day to children? "No!" We need to turn our nos into yesses. When your darling is mucking about in the plants, instead of saying "No, don't touch!" you can say, "Here, play with this," as you offer a toy. Most toddlers respond well to diversion.

Parents also spend a lot of time giving orders. "Don't run!" "No, don't eat in the living room." We can turn this around and tell our children what they *can* do rather than saying no. "When we go shopping you can sit in the cart and hold the cereal box for me," instead of "When we go shopping, don't touch anything."

Our homes are often filled with no-nos. Plants, breakables, purses, electronic equipment; all this wonderful, interesting stuff that a child is constantly drawn to and parents are constantly yelling, "No, don't touch that!" Babyproofing your home solves this problem. Toddlers are naturally curious and we do them a real favor when we allow them to roam freely in an environment filled with yesses.

Toddlers are also trying to reach a first level of independence and want to assert themselves. Saying no gives them some power. If we give them many opportunities to succeed, they will become more positive. So besides babyproofing, small stools to allow them to reach, toys that are accessible, Velcro shoes etc. make life more positive for junior.

Chapter 4

DISCIPLINE
THE BEDROCK OF CHARACTER

CHILDREN MISBEHAVE, PARENTS DISCIPLINE. SOUNDS EASY ENOUGH. And it is easy — for those who've never had to do it. There's Kevin in the supermarket line-up screaming his head off and everyone is watching. What's a parent to do? In the heat of the moment, disappearing seems like the only reasonable option!

When children misbehave we're rarely at our best, not often calm, rational or thoughtful. At that point we will respond automatically and do with Kevin what was done with us when we were children. This is fine, unless what was done with us was insufficient or counterproductive, possibly even abusive, and we've decided we need to do it differently.

It is also easy to lose the ability to separate our personal issues, problems and feelings from our children's behavior. We see ourselves reflected in their behavior and react instinctively. Not always the best move.

This is where our long-term goal-setting really kicks in. This tantrum is inappropriate and disrespectful not only to you, but to all the folks in the line-up. What does he need to learn and what is the best way to teach it? Is this a case that calls for punishment? No, it calls for discipline. And there's a world of difference between discipline and punishment.

DISCIPLINE VS. PUNISHMENT

Punishment is about causing pain or discomfort in an effort to change behavior. We hurt a child so that he will think twice about misbehaving again. And it often works — in the short term. It works as long as we hurt him enough to dissuade him from repeating the misbehavior. We typically think of punishment as being physical, as in smacking or spanking. However, threatening, belittling, insulting, frightening or humiliating children is also punishment. And it works only as long as a child is afraid of his parents. All the motivation is external. Children learn that parents will hurt them if they don't follow the rules, but they don't learn why those rules exist. Instead, they learn to be sneaky so they won't get caught, and that they can misbehave when nobody's watching. We've all heard about teens who throw parties as soon as their parents are away.

Spanking — which is simply a euphemism for hitting — is such an integral part of our history of child-raising it deserves a special mention. Some parents argue that spanking is an effective punishment because it can get the child's immediate attention

and stop the offensive behavior. And it often does. However, there are two problems with this parenting strategy.

First, children who do stop misbehaving are doing so because they are afraid that their parent, a much bigger person, will hurt them. So pain and fear are the motivators. As the child gets older the fear of pain diminishes, so she takes the licking and carries on doing whatever she wants to do. Children who are spanked do not learn to do the right thing — they learn to avoid or disregard pain. And they do not learn how to take responsibility for the real consequences of their misbehavior. They get hit, it's all over, and the slate is wiped clean.

What do they learn? That's the second problem. As we saw in Chapter 3 (Mirror Images), children learn by observation and mimic the behavior of adults. So when we hit our kids, we teach them that hitting someone smaller is an appropriate response to anger or frustration.

So how is discipline different?

Discipline is not about pain or punishment, nor about revenge or retribution. Discipline is about teaching, guiding and training. When we discipline children we are teaching them the difference between right and wrong. We're helping them to learn about the consequences of their actions. We are developing children of character. They learn why rules exist and how breaking the rules impacts on others as well as themselves. They slowly internalize the information so they can behave appropriately in future.

Fine words, but how do we do this? You start with a strong foundation, which is the family's rules and expectations. These are developed based on the values you've identified and the long-term goals you've set. Initially, you determine the basic family rules and outline behaviors that are expected. These commonly include being respectful of others and co-operating to make the family unit work

Once the basic foundation is in place, each family can build a discipline plan to suit its needs, and make the required adjustments as children grow and mature. There are several logical steps to child discipline. Following them makes it more straightforward for both you and your children. When a child misbehaves, we sometimes find ourselves arbitrarily reaching out for the first consequence that comes to mind. But if this choice doesn't fit into any long-term plan and doesn't consider the age of the child or the circumstances, we've created another problem for ourselves.

STEP ONE: PREVENTION

Depending on her age, the first and most important step is to prevent some of the more predictable misbehaviors. Some behavior is simply a child's way of letting us know that some aspect of her day-to-day life just isn't working for her. She can't just come to us and say, "You know, the way you have the back entry set up works against us kids. We're just too short to reach the hooks. Now, if you made a change we could stop all these problems about our coats and mittens being on the floor." Children can't tell us what's bothering them so they fuss, they refuse to go to bed, they cry or they create an uproar. If we can anticipate the situations which will cause this reaction and respond to the child's needs, we can prevent the misbehavior from happening in the first place.

Every parent is familiar with the childproofing that occurs when toddlers start getting mobile. We childproof the house so no harm can happen. If we take that example and extend it to other aspects of our children's lives, we spare our children and ourselves a lot of grief and aggravation. For example, seven-year-old Nathan likes to take his time in the morning. This leads to a confrontation every day when he's just not ready to leave for school on time. Rather than nagging at him, simply having him get up 15 minutes earlier can solve the problem — and maintain both his dignity and your sanity.

Even unusually challenging situations can often be managed with a little planning. You're going to visit your elderly Aunt Rose on Sunday. She loves your kids but can't stand any noise. You just know the kids are going to get in trouble. It's going to be a nightmare.

So, you take the kids to the park on your way to Aunt Rose's home. The kids get rid of all their pent-up energy before they arrive for the visit. You bring some favorite quiet-play toys, and you make it a short stay, leaving before the kids become bored. This way everyone has a good visit!

STEP TWO: CAN YOU DO NOTHING?

Not all misbehaviors can be prevented, but some are self-correcting: they simply take care of themselves. Ask yourself, "What would happen naturally if I did nothing?" If you've been in the habit of saving your children from the consequences of their actions, you may discover that you can sometimes stay out of it and let your children handle the consequences on their own.

You notice that your daughter has once again forgotten to take her gym clothes to school. Normally you'd run them up to her to save her from the teacher's wrath. But what if you did nothing and let her take responsibility for her own carelessness? Mind you, if you've been saving her for years, first warn her that the good times are over and she's now expected to handle her own school stuff. Children learn a lot from experience. Let her learn from the experience of dealing with the teacher.

STEP THREE: GIVE NATURE A NUDGE

In many situations, doing nothing isn't an option. The natural consequence is dangerous or just plain unacceptable. So you want to give nature a nudge. What would happen naturally? How closely can you approximate the natural consequence?

Timothy and his sister are having an argument. Timothy grabs a cushion and throws it at his sister, Deborah. She retaliates and the fight is on. A cushion hits a vase of flowers, causing a real mess of water, flowers and broken glass. What should their parents do?

Denying them TV for three days may get their attention, but that would be punishment. It won't teach them why rough play in the living room is not permitted. Having them clean up the mess and contributing money toward a new vase will. The amount of money they contribute can be determined by their ages and the amount of money they can reasonably raise.

Dealing with child misbehavior takes thought and planning. The clearer you are, the easier it will be. When your children know that you have a plan and will follow it, they're more likely to behave because they know the consequences of misbehavior. When the consequences make sense, children learn why we have certain rules.

POWER STRUGGLES

"Get out of power struggles."

That's what the books, the courses and experts all say. Unfortunately, they don't always tell you *how*.

Let's start at the beginning. What is a power struggle? A power struggle exists in a conflict when the issue becomes winning and each party to the conflict is focused only on that. Each person stands his ground, unwilling to budge, and tries to force the other to move.

In a power struggle the real issue gets lost in the need to win. Power struggles often end in stalemates. Even when they don't, no one really wins because the relationship suffers so badly. A parent may "win" power struggles with a child because she can physically move him. He'll either submit and know that he's a loser or decide that although his parents can pick him up, they can't control his thoughts. He'll say or think; "Just wait until I'm bigger."

If the parent's goal is the short-term one of changing the behavior immediately, she'll define herself as a winner.

But the long-term goals — directing and teaching the child about acceptable behavior, helping him to have high self-esteem and to be independent, building a strong relationship between parent and child — those will all suffer.

Then there is the lazy way: Avoid dealing with the situation and simply give up. This is a trap created by misinterpreting the advice to stay out of power struggles. Staying out of a power struggle does *not* mean ignoring the behavior and allowing the child to continue doing whatever she wants. It means breaking the tension, changing the focus. It means changing your own motivation from needing to win ("I'll show this kid! If he thinks he can do this to me ...") back to your larger discipline goals ("This is not acceptable behavior; Jeffrey needs to learn that when he acts in that way he can't participate in family activities").

How?

The more your family has developed a positive approach to discipline, the less likely you are to be dealing with power struggles.

However, that doesn't make you immune and at certain times conflict will escalate and you will find yourself embroiled almost before you know it. You will know you are in a power struggle when all you can think about is winning. If you want to deal with the issue and try to salvage the self-esteem of both your child and yourself, you will first have to break the struggle and refocus.

The best way to do that is to physically separate — even for a minute. A trip to the bathroom is a beautiful way to accomplish this. You can leave the scene and return without losing face or giving in. But the break does give everyone a chance to regroup and a new and more positive approach can be tried when you return. (This is equally effective when engaged in a power struggle with another adult.)

Sometimes a bit of exercise helps: "I think we need to clear our heads. I'm going for a walk around the block, then we can continue this discussion."

You can also suggest a time-out: "Look, we're getting nowhere right now. Let's discuss this after supper."

Let's look at how this might play out in real life. It's time for Janelle to go to bed. You've asked her to put on her pyjamas and she refuses. You reach to grab her and force her into her pjs; she is sitting firmly on the bed determined to stay in her clothes. You are face to face, heading for a real confrontation, when suddenly the phone rings. You leave the room to answer it and your conversation with a friend allows you to calm down. Now you are able to return to Janelle's room and handle the pyjama issue with some maturity.

It is likely that the mere action of your leaving the room allowed Janelle to get ready for bed without losing face. After all, sitting all alone on the bed being stubborn can get boring in a real hurry. In that case, you can be matter-of-fact as you kiss her good night. If she is still dressed you can say something like; "It's bedtime. Do you want to wear your clothes or your pyjamas?" or "I know you can get into your pyjamas now so why don't I just tidy the bathroom while you get ready for bed."

Remember, staying out of power struggles doesn't mean ignoring your child's misbehavior. It doesn't mean letting him do whatever he wants and it doesn't mean standing by helpless in the face of his decisions.

It means re-focusing, re-directing and dealing with the issue. It means working toward a solution to the problem, not winning. And in this way everyone wins. But, it's hard work!

How to Break a Power Struggle
- Announce that you have to go to the bathroom
- Suggest you take a break and re-visit the discussion at a set time
- Stop for a snack
- Go out and run around the block

IN OTHER WORDS...

Effective child discipline helps children internalize the reasons for rules and limits. It teaches them respect for those around them. They learn that there are expected standards of behavior in their family, school and community.

Discipline has an important role to play in developing children of character. Children who have learned right from wrong, and can imagine the consequences of their actions, are well-equipped to stand up and do the right thing.

Talking about Behavior
Kathy's Q & A

QUESTION
My 18-month-old son Darryl will not sit down to eat. He stands on his booster seat and tries to get onto the table. What can I do to get him to sit long enough to eat something?

ANSWER
Getting an 18-month-old to sit still is often like trying to launch a space ship with a match. Is he eating with the rest of the family? If he's eating alone you will likely have more problems. He loves to be part of the family activity and this includes mealtimes. While you're all at the table make sure to include him in the con-

versation. Often toddlers who are disruptive at the table are simply bored and tired of being ignored. They want to be part of the socialization that's taking place.

With a toddler it's a good idea to have his plate prepared and ready to eat before calling him to the table. That way he can get right to the business at hand without having to wait. Don't expect him to stay at the table as long as you do. Once he's finished let him down.

He also needs to learn about basic manners. So, when he stands on his seat offer him a choice that he either sit in his seat or leave the table. If he gets up again simply remove him and let him know he can return when he's ready to sit. You don't need to send him to another room, just down from the table. If he wants back immediately, let him up and assume he's ready to sit still.

When he's simply fooling around, he's finished eating so clear his plate from the table and carry on with your meal. Don't worry about the amount of food he eats. Toddlers often seem to eat very little and thrive. As long as he's active and healthy, he's fine.

QUESTION

My mother recently gave me some parenting advice. She told me never to say, "Do you want…" or "Would you like to…?" Instead, tell the child what to do without giving a choice. I can see many consequences, good and bad to using this approach.

What's your opinion?

ANSWER

Offering children choices is a recent parenting trend. It's a trend I applaud but is also one that is often misunderstood.

Your mother has probably seen some children who are being permitted to make all their own choices with no direction. When parents interpret offering choices to mean that a child can do anything she wants, that is not healthy.

More typically it's easy to fall into the habit of offering a choice when none exists — for example, "Do you want to go home now?" If you have decided it's time to go home from the park or after a visit with friends, it's not a choice. You might say instead, "We need to leave now, do you want to hold my hand or walk beside me?"

It's also easy to over-use the concept. Children do not need to be making choices constantly. Sometimes a simple "Let's go, it's time to leave" does the trick.

However, when we offer our children appropriate choices, they develop a feeling of competence and learn that we trust them and will respect their decisions. Making a bad choice is a great learning experience. For example, if nine-year-old Kelsey decides to bring her doll along when she goes to the mall with her mom, she may soon learn that having to carry it around all afternoon is a challenge. Next time she'll think about the situation and what's more appropriate in the circumstances.

Children need limits, rules and direction. When you offer a choice, you give the child an opportunity to exercise some personal power in his life. But offer choices within the limits that are already acceptable within your home. For example, with a preschooler it's better to say, "Here are two play outfits, which one would you like to wear?" than "What do you want to wear today?" Once she is older and knows the difference between her play clothes and good outfits, she can choose without your help.

Telling a child what to do without giving a choice can easily lead to power struggles as the child gets older. You tell him what to do and he says, "No!" Then what? Offering a choice takes away the option of saying no. He has a choice to either do this or do that.

This is a great time for you to be developing a discipline plan for you and your child. You might want to consider taking a parenting course to help you with the process.

QUESTION

How do I deal with a rebel four-year-old stepchild? I've tried almost everything, please help!

ANSWER

Parenting a stepchild carries with it many challenges and frustrations.

This four-year-old probably resents your presence in his life. He wants his mom and dad, and he wants them together. Generally, it's preferable to have his biological parent be the primary caregiver and disciplinarian. So try to reduce your parenting role for the time being. This will reassure him that you're not trying to take his other parent's place.

He may be causing you problems because it's safe. He's less willing to risk the displeasure of his parents because he's afraid of losing them, so you become the target of his fears, insecurities and anger.

He needs permission to be angry. Let him express his anger in acceptable ways, through physical activity or simply talking about it. But be aware that while four-year-olds are quite verbal, they are not subtle. So don't take his anger personally. He's angry at the break-up of his family — you are simply the proof that his parents' marriage is over.

How is his relationship with both biological parents? He needs his mother and his father and his behavior toward you may be a signal that he's feeling the loss of one of them. If he has contact with his other parent, talk about him or her, have lots of pictures around and give him permission to talk to you about both his mom and his dad.

The issue of love is also a common stumbling block. Because you love his parent, you may believe you should love the child. You do not need to love this child nor does he need to love you. Respect, caring and simple good manners are essential but love may or may not grow between you.

Finally, four-year-olds can be challenging at the best of times. Try to appreciate his energy and give him the time he needs to get to know you.

QUESTION

I have a nine-year-old grandchild who whines constantly. He also refuses to take responsibility for his behavior. For example, he spilled a drink right in front of his mom then said he didn't do it.

She has tried everything: talking, rewards, grounding, time-outs, you name it.

His parents are divorced and his father sees him infrequently. We know that hurts the boy. My daughter has tried to talk to the father and explain how he's hurting his son, but he won't listen.

ANSWER

This is a very unhappy boy. For starters, you want to find him some counseling to deal with his issues around his father. Usually, I don't deal with questions when there is therapy involved, but there are some other general parenting concerns here. It's not okay for him to use his parent's divorce as an excuse for misbehavior. He definitely needs help because he's hurting, but once you've found him a good child psychologist, he needs some quality parenting.

You mention that his mother has tried everything and that might be the problem. She needs to develop a parenting style and stick to it. I'd recommend that she find a parenting education program and take it. That will help her learn some parenting techniques in an educational and supportive environment.

Whining can be extraordinarily annoying. Trying to ignore it is almost impossible for most of us. A more effective strategy is to talk to him when he's not whining about his proper voice and his whiney voice, and let him know that you really hate to listen when he whines. Then when he does whine simply say "I just can't listen to that" and leave the room or turn away from him. As soon as his voice changes pay attention to him.

In terms of refusing to take responsibility for his behavior, I'd suggest that his mother forget about assessing blame and move to problem-solving. When he spills his milk, she can say: "Look at this mess, let's clean it up," and hand him a cloth. If he answers that it isn't his fault, she can say that it doesn't matter, what matters is that there is a mess and it needs cleaning. He needs to learn that it's not about blame; it's about taking responsibility to solve the problem.

Finally, your daughter should stop trying to talk to her ex-husband. He's not listening and it's just frustrating her. She can only control what happens between her and her son.

Chapter 5

PARENTING TEENS
YES, YOU'RE STILL IMPORTANT

BARBARA AND GORDON WERE VISITING WITH THEIR FRIENDS Sheila and Ken one Saturday night. As both couples have children, the conversation turned to the kids. Sheila and Ken's kids were off visiting their grandparents for the weekend. They are eight and ten years of age and love to go stay with their relatives from time to time. When Barbara and Gordon heard about this they looked at each other and then said to their friends, "Just you wait. Our kids are now teenagers and there's no way they'd go visit their grandparents."

"So, what are they up to tonight?" Ken asked.

"We haven't a clue," Barbara said. "They do whatever they want and we just don't know what's going on."

"Typical teens!" Gordon sighed.

The next week Sheila and Ken attended a parenting workshop and asked me if it was inevitable that all teens just run wild. As I thought about it, I realized that I often hear reports of teens doing whatever they want.

"She's 14 years old. She's going to make her own decisions and there's nothing I can do about it but pray."

"He's 15 and totally ruled by hormones. There's nothing I can say or do if I see him making bad choices."

"By the time they're teenagers, they're raised. A parent can only stand by and watch and maybe be a friend."

These are comments I've recently heard from friends and workshop participants and I have one response:

Poppycock!

Teens behave as if they don't want or need their parents and too many parents today are buying it. In his excellent book *Hear Me, Hug Me, Trust Me*, Dr. G. Scott Wooding points out that "while teens may be more knowledgeable, and often more physically and emotionally tense, their emotional needs and control valves are no different than we their parents at an equivalent age."

Over four years, Dr. Wooding, a counselor and teacher in a junior high school, asked students to write down the characteristics of an ideal parent. He expected to see characteristics such as generous with allowance and slack on rules. But teens are smarter than that: they know what they need. Four years of questionnaires came down to 12 suggestions to parents from teens.

They want parents who care. They want us to understand their issues, improve communication, provide appropriate discipline, help them develop responsibility and demonstrate trust. They want us to be fair, respectful and honest. A sense of humor, spending time together and being an appropriate role model were also included.

When people ask me, "What's the matter with teens today?" my answer is likely to be that they're missing the supervision, direction and stability they need to get on with the task of reaching adulthood. Teenagers are our children. They may be big, outspoken and quite independent but they are our children and we are their parents. Teenagers not only need parents and parenting, they need it desperately. But parenting teens is different from raising younger children.

It is typical and healthy for teens to be separating from their parents and achieving increased independence. Remember when your child was a toddler, stating with absolute assurance, "I can do it myself!" You knew he wanted to do everything for himself, but you also knew he just couldn't. Your job was to help him to do what he could and create a safe environment while he grew from an infant to a preschooler.

Our role is identical with teens. They need a safe environment from which to launch themselves into adulthood. Like their younger selves, they can become victims of their own impulses and desire to be independent.

Teens need to have input into the family rules, to be consulted and heard. But this doesn't mean there should be no rules, no bottom-line, no clear expectations.

When Rebecca was three, she was with her parents or a caregiver at all times — they always knew where she was. In elementary school she started participating in extracurricular activities and was sometimes out at soccer practice, at Brownies, or at a friend's. Her parents, though, still knew where she was, who she was with, and when she was coming home.

Now that Rebecca's a teenager she may be out with her friends and her parents are not always sure what she's up to. But they still make sure they know where she is going and when she'll be home. Their method has changed since she was little, though. These days they sit down together and negotiate the rules.

If you're clear on your basic, bottom-line rules (never getting into a car with a driver who has been drinking, for example), then you can listen to your teen's plans and work toward an agreement that meets both your needs. When she sees that you will listen and that you're fair, the process can be positive.

Parenting teens can be frustrating but also joyous and exhilarating. Give your teens the gift of leadership and the security of knowing they have the support and guidance of you their parents.

IN OTHER WORDS...

Teens need limits, supervision and rules just as much as younger children do. Parenting teens requires negotiation, discussion and flexibility. As they mature we change the method, but not the action, of parenting our children.

Talking about Behavior
Kathy's Q & A

QUESTION

I have two children, aged 12 and 14. They call me at the office when they get home from school just to check in. Some of my colleagues say that they're too old to have to do this. They say I'm not letting them grow up. What do you think?

ANSWER

Having your children check in with you isn't about letting them grow up. It's about family members touching base. The kids have been in school all day and just want to say hello. It is not about independence, it's about communication. This gives you an opportunity to spend a few minutes with each of your children on a daily basis.

It's also reassuring. Once our children are beyond after-school child care we like to know that they're home and safe. Although most parents trust their children, they still worry. And our children, much as they complain, don't mind a certain amount of worry. They know it means we care about them.

At certain stages teens can be quite emotional and if something is bothering them it's immediate. When they can talk to you right after school, they can get advice or a friendly ear. It also prepares you for what you might have to help them with that evening.

With today's busy families, no matter how well you plan, schedules change. A phone call can be the time for altering plans if necessary.

Mainly though it's just nice. It's nice to take a few minutes in the afternoon to chat with your kids.

QUESTION

My 15-year-old daughter wants to go a party next weekend. The problem is that there will be no adults there. I don't think she should attend an unsupervised party; she says I don't trust her. What do you think?

ANSWER

I'm with you. Going to this party is a bad idea.

Unsupervised parties are catalysts for all kinds of trouble. She probably has a group of very nice, trustworthy friends. But an unsupervised party is too tempting for teens.

Once the word gets out, there are likely to be gatecrashers. The young host is unlikely to be able to keep them out. Soon the size of the party can escalate out of control.

Liquor is another problem. Some of the kids are going to see this as a great chance to drink or use drugs.

Your daughter is probably not going to respond well to your concerns. She'll say that her friends don't act like that, that they won't tell anyone else about the party and that you should trust her.

You need to be clear that unsupervised parties are not for her. Period. Don't try to rationalize or argue. It just won't work.

There is also the possibility that she needs you to say no. Otherwise why would she tell you that there is no supervision? She isn't quite mature enough to tell her friends that she isn't comfortable going, so she's using you to make the decision. Then she can blame it on her mean parents and still stay safely at home.

On party night she may be open to having a few friends over to your home. Or she may still be angry and spend the night on the phone (with her other friends who weren't allowed to go) complaining about you.

You simply need to be clear that you're making the right decision and refuse to argue. Good luck.

QUESTION

My 12-year-old daughter's room is a real mess. I'm tired of fighting with her to clean it up. I would just close the door and forget about it, but I'm concerned that would send the message that it's okay to be messy and disorganized. What do you suggest?

ANSWER

Messy bedrooms are a source of conflict in many families. Adults and children have very different views of what constitutes clean. It's clean enough for her and she just can't understand what all the fuss is about.

The first task is to make sure she knows how to clean her room. This will probably involve a joint cleaning session and I would recommend using lots of containers and shelves to hold her things.

Once it's clean and tidy and you're certain she has the skills, stay out of it. It is her personal space and she may be much happier amongst clutter. But you can have some rules, such as no food left lying around. Explain that food attracts bugs that can crawl under the door and invade the rest of the house.

She will learn about the need to be organized and neat by how you keep the rest of the house. It's perfectly acceptable to set higher standards for neatness in the common areas such as the living room and kitchen.

If you absolutely can't allow yourself to simply close her door, negotiate a level of order and time of cleaning with her. It may be that you'd like her to do a clean-up every week or two, so the room can be vacuumed. Whatever you choose, make sure the two of you decide together.

Clean bedrooms aren't worth major battles, so try to keep it in perspective.

QUESTION

I have a three-year-old and want to see her become an independent and confident person. How can I best do that?

ANSWER

Children acquire independence as a process. It begins with their first breath and continues until the day they leave home. We allow them to make steps toward complete independence as they're ready throughout their childhood.

Toddlers can be asked to help carry a can of peas from the car to the house and place it in a low cupboard. A preschooler can help put away more groceries and by elementary school they are even being trusted with the eggs. High school students can carry in and put away groceries on their own and once they have a driver's license can do the shopping. It's a process.

We also teach children to become independent when we allow them to make choices. Eleven-year-old Jessica may choose to leave her bike lying on the driveway. You have already spoken to her about how to care for it. She has a safe place to leave it and a good lock. If you decide to get her bike and lock it up you're doing nothing to help her. Even the subsequent lecture is unlikely to change her behavior. Alternately you could choose to put her bike away for a few days and let her know that by neglecting to care for it she's lost the right to use it. If she still leaves her bike out frequently, you could simply ignore it and have her deal with the consequences should it be stolen or run over. Both of these strategies will help her learn to consider the consequences of her behavior, and lead to adult independence and self-reliance.

Carrying on a conversation is another important skill. When I was a girl I was expected to meet and greet every guest in our home no matter what age. I was expected to say hello and engage in a little chitchat before I returned to my play. I had the same expectations for my children and as a result they have developed into young adults ready to speak to anyone.

Healthy discussion and debate around the dinner table is another great source of positive development. In this safe environment, children learn how to agree and disagree, how to make their point and how to listen to others. Encourage your daughter to express her thoughts and opinions, and respect her point of view.

The rule of thumb is to let your three-year-old do, decide and discover what she can for herself as soon as she's ready. Let her take responsibility for her decisions and actions, both positive and negative. Encourage her in each stage of development and odds are she will be an independent self-assured young lady when she leaves the nest.

QUESTION

Our 14-year-old granddaughter needs to wear prescription glasses. However, she claims she just cannot bring herself to wear them and simply refuses to do so.

She is a pretty girl, well adjusted and a good student. Her glasses are stylish and modern and other family members wear glasses. It's obvious that she needs to wear hers in order to see well enough while in school, watching TV or even at sports activities.

Everybody — teachers, parents, grandparents (us!) — is patiently waiting for her to change her mind. Do you think this is a reasonable and healthy approach?

ANSWER

Just waiting isn't going to solve this problem. You need to find out why she won't wear them. I imagine you have probably been explaining to her the reasons why she should wear them: "If you don't wear your glasses you won't do well in school and your marks will go down. You don't want that, do you?" It makes sense to us.

Ask her why she won't wear them. Then be quiet and listen. Don't debate any of her comments. Just respond by saying, "Uh-huh — and what else?" Then listen some more. If you're patient you may be surprised at her reasons.

It could be that kids in glasses are teased a lot in her circle of friends, or maybe something as simple as they hurt her nose. Once you know what's happening you can help her work to a solution.

She does, however, have to wear them. A trip to her doctor for an explanation might help. Certainly, her parents can tell her that she can't watch TV, go to movies or attend sports games without them because that will damage her eyes.

Have you considered contact lenses? Maybe you can give her lenses as a gift.

Chapter 6

IF YOUR KIDS DON'T SOMETIMES HATE YOU, YOU'RE NOT DOING YOUR JOB
THE TOUGH WORK OF PARENTING

"MEANIE."

"You don't love me!"

"Everything was going along fine, and now I'm having a horrible day — thanks to you!"

"I hate you!"

None of us like to see our child unhappy or angry. Nobody likes to be cast in the role of the Mean Parent. But sometimes being a good parent means standing firm, following through, or demanding that our kids take responsibility for their own choices — and being prepared to weather the storm that may follow. These are the times when we have to remind ourselves that parenting is not a popularity contest — it's a job. Sometimes, it's a tough job.

In my workshops and keynote addresses parents talk to me about their frustrations. They are caring, considerate and responsible people working hard to raise healthy children. They believe they're doing all the right things, but it's just not working. Because society and family life have changed so dramatically in recent decades, their parents aren't much help — many parenting practices from earlier generations are simply no longer appropriate.

So, what's going on?

In some cases, parents are taking a good idea, like explaining rules, and carrying it to extremes. In others, they are using ineffective, but easy, strategies to avoid the hard work that's really required to help children grow into responsible, caring, self-sufficient adults.

SEVEN POPULAR PARENTING STRATEGIES THAT JUST DON'T WORK

These are strategies that I'm seeing from parents who care enough about child-raising to attend my workshops or listen to my radio program. They have read and heard about new ideas about parenting that seem to fit better with today's values or our busy lives. Trouble is, they just don't work.

No parent makes all these mistakes, all the time. But many of us fall into these traps at least some of the time. So take a look. Do you see yourself in any of these pictures?

Explaining

"I will never say to my child, you'll do it because I said so." We don't want to see our children being raised to be mindlessly obedient and to do what they're told without understanding the reasons. Explaining the rules and expectations helps our children to learn why we do what we do. They can understand that decisions are not always simple and that there are often unseen long-term consequences to our choices.

Which is all very well and good, but over-explaining can easily backfire.

First, our explanations are often far too complex for young children. While a short, simple reason is fine, they are too little to understand long explanations. They aren't ready to follow and act on adult logic. Toddlers and preschoolers are waiting to see what we're going to do. While we talk, they wait. We can explain to three-year-old Olivia that she must sit in her car seat because it's safe. We can even talk about what might happen in an accident if she were sitting with just a regular seat belt. But until we actually put her in the seat or give her the choice to sit in her car seat or stay home, she just won't get it.

I talk to a lot of parents who believe that if we explain the situation, the kids will automatically change their behavior to meet our needs. The reality often is that the children aren't even sure what is being asked of them.

Five-year-old Shayla runs into the house in her muddy shoes and races into the kitchen, leaving dirty footprints in her wake. Her mom rushes in and says, "Shayla, I just washed that floor."

"Oh," is the neutral response as Shayla continues on her way, making even more mess.

"Shayla, I just washed that floor!" her mom shrieks as she grabs her, takes her to the back door and removes the offending shoes. Shayla still doesn't get it.

If her mom had said, "Shayla, shoes off now. I just washed that floor and you're making a mess," the five-year-old would know what to do and why. But she just didn't get the connection between the job her mom had done (so she washed the floor, so what, who cares, certainly not Shayla who's keen to get into the house), and the behavior that was required.

You need to tell her in simple language exactly what you need from her.

Finally, children quickly learn that they can forestall their parents by asking questions, and then more questions. If we're determined to explain we will keep talking. Half an hour later, instead of going to bed or walking the dog, the kids have us deep into a discussion of "what's fair." If they manage to outlast us (and kids have *lots* of patience for fruitless discussion!), we may well end up letting them off the hook: "Oh, forget it! I'll walk the damn dog myself!"

Lecturing is easy. Dealing with a child who is unhappy is not. But if we truly want to help our children, we need to help them to experience what will happen to them as a result of misbehavior.

Explaining, then throwing up our hands in despair when our children do not respond in the way we had hoped, doesn't work. Parents who refuse to deal with an unhappy child who does not, at that moment, "love" them are parents who are neglecting the work of parenting.

Excuses

When 11-year-old Jared started a fight in the schoolyard, the consequence was a three-day suspension. Despite Jared's history of misbehavior at school, his parents showed up at the meeting with the school principal armed with excuses. Jared is small for his age, they said, so he always has to prove himself. They insisted he was not responsible and that he should be placed in a different school because now he was embarrassed. They went to the district superintendent of schools and the school board.

Jared's parents love him and are trying to be the best parents they can be. They believe that it's their job to support their son — which it is. They think they are doing this by taking his part against the school. But how does that support Jared's long-term growth? Making excuses for him teaches him that he doesn't have to take responsibility for his behavior. So those excuses aren't doing Jared any good. They do, however, offer an "easy way out" to his parents. Otherwise, he's likely to make their lives miserable while he deals with the consequences of his inappropriate behavior.

Working with the teacher to support the mandated suspension and helping Jared learn to control his behavior is what's really needed here. Jared needs all the adults in his life to work together to help him learn how to behave in a way that is responsible and appropriate.

Parents today want to understand their children and why they act the way they do — and that's a good thing. So naturally, parents look for the reasons to explain their child's negative behavior. Some of the reasons I hear from parents in my groups include:

"We moved recently and she's upset."

"She just started school."

"She's had a cold."

Sometimes these reasons are legitimate, but they don't necessarily excuse the behavior. On the one hand, responsible parents need to be aware of the needs of their child based on the situation, and should offer whatever help the child requires. On the other hand, parents must teach that misbehavior is not an acceptable response to adversity.

Ten-year-old Jonathan has been miserable since he started in his new school two weeks ago. He sulks through dinner and fights with his brother every morning before he has to leave. Now, moving and attending a new school is difficult for most children. Jonathan's parents can decide that he has a reason for his behavior and simply let him carry on, or they can help him to make this challenging transition.

Helping him starts with letting him know that you're aware that this is a difficult time for him but the way he's handling it just isn't acceptable. Sulking through dinner can be replaced by talking about his struggles to fit in. Without dismissing his concerns, Jonathan's parents can help by encouraging him to consider ways to overcome the problems. "Have you thought about joining the chess club? You really enjoyed that at your last school."

His parents might also talk to the teacher to ask for assistance. Possibly the teacher has identified a potential friend for Jonathan and could partner them in a project.

It's a serious trap for parents to always find an excuse for misbehavior. Parents who use explanations and excuses to protect their children are in fact handicapping them — even when the reasons are real. Children need to learn skills to enable them to cope with both the good and bad aspects of life. Parents need to help their children to develop these skills and they need to understand that sometimes, in this process, their children will not be very happy.

Attention

Children need our attention. Children also want our attention.

Their need for attention can immobilize parents. If, the thinking goes, my child is demanding my attention it's because she's not getting enough and that's my fault.

So, it becomes another excuse.

"My child is misbehaving. It is because she needs attention. Therefore I will spend the next week spending all my time with the child, doing whatever she wants. I will be patient and understanding and after receiving this attention, my child will start to feel wanted and loved and will change her behavior."

The trick is to maintain a balance. Caring parents (and if you're reading this book you fit into that category) do pay attention to their children. What flummoxes us is that we give them attention and still they want more.

When I think about this I think about potato chips or peanuts. It's pretty difficult to eat just one. We want to keep eating as long as we can. Attention is the same — we want as much as we can get. Why not? It feels good.

It's okay to say, "Not now dear, I'm busy. I'll play with you later; meanwhile I'm sure you can find something to do."

We can also give our kids the attention they need while getting on with our busy days. They love to be included. Working with children is a way of connecting that is often sadly neglected. If you're doing the laundry, the little ones love to fold small items like underwear, preschoolers can pair socks while older kids can fold and put away. The work gets done and you have time to chat and tell stories.

But giving kids your loving attention does not replace the work of discipline. Children need both.

Quality Time

Quality Time — the concept of making sure that the limited time you spend with your children is of high quality — took the parenting world by storm in the mid-'80s. There were articles describing ways to make 20 minutes with your child a valuable and memorable time.

A 15-year-old reading an article on the topic said, "It sounds to me like an excuse to spend hardly any time with your kids and not feel guilty."

Right on. Every time I think this concept is dead it rears its ugly head again. Children need our time. They need boring time, quiet time, working together time, being in the same room engaged in different activities time, physical care time, discipline time, discussion time, story time. They need us. They need to know that we will give them the time they need as much as we possibly can.

Quality Time is a crock.

Being there when they need us is responsible parenting. This doesn't mean we need to be with them physically at all times. Obviously you can't always be with them. But you can let them know that you're thinking of them. Dual-income families or employed single parents can stay in touch by phone. Some parents have told me that they plan their coffee break to match the time their kids get home from school so they can touch base. Many employed parents make sure that the receptionist knows who their children are and that they are to be informed if the kids call. If at all possible, try to arrange to leave work early to watch important sporting events or school concerts. In these ways we let children know that when they need us, we'll be there.

Programming

There is a dizzying array of opportunities now for children to experience any number of activities from a very young age. Busy parents who want their children to have the chance to participate in sports, the arts or music can simply enroll them in a program. It's a great chance for them to try out a range of activities.

The problem comes when your child is overprogrammed. You find yourself taking your child from school to one activity followed by dinner in the car followed by an evening program. When there are too many activities at once, the children are moved like so many packages from one enrichment activity to another.

There is a myth that if children are to excel in an activity they need to start at a young age. But the reality is that most of us *don't* excel, and what's more we don't need to: we just do our best and have fun. So a child can learn to swim and enjoy the water for the rest of his life, but never enter a race. On the other hand, it is also possible to excel in a sport or activity and start at a later age.

The problem with overprogramming is that children also need free time. They need time to dream, to run and play, to help their parents cook, clean and make home repairs. They need time to ask questions, to study and to just hang around alone and with their friends, not doing much of anything. We are a very activity-focused society and often feel that free time is wasted time. Quite the opposite is true. Free time is the home of creative thought; it allows your child to just let her mind wander and wonder about the world. It also teaches her how to spend some time with herself, so she learns to be self-directed rather than "bored" by unscripted time. It lets her rest and gain extra energy.

For young kids, free time requires adult supervision and in some cases adult involvement; programming only requires registration and a parent who doesn't mind doing a lot of driving. It's all about maintaining a balance.

Martyr

Martyrdom is the mainstay of many situation comedies. It's a joke, but like many jokes it has its basis in truth. Parents make sacrifices for their children, that's a given. Some parents just do what needs to be done, staying home and missing a party because a child is sick or buying a backpack for him for school rather than a new purse for herself. For most this is a simple reality of being a parent.

But in some families it's not so simple. The children are made aware of every sacrifice made by the parent. The motivation isn't nasty; these parents want their children to learn what has been done for them, to be grateful. A laudable goal, but it's not in keeping with child development. Children are self-centered beings, busy with the tasks associated with growing up. When their parents let them know about the sacrifices they have made, everything from dropping out of university to going without a new dress, children simply feel guilty and aren't sure where to put it. They can't do anything to change the situation, but they feel badly that they are the source of their parents' unhappiness. They will become aware and grateful in a decade or two, but meanwhile just need parents who do the best they can under the circumstances.

Then there is the busy martyr. There is so much that needs to be done in the community, and this parent does it all: coaches sports, sits on the school parent committee, volunteers for every event. All laudable and important, but commitments need to be kept in moderation to protect family time. What makes her not only busy but a martyr is that she complains constantly about her schedule. But the children can't complain as their mother rushes off to yet another meeting or drags them along to help with the bake sale, because everything she does is "for them." The average child is usually thinking; "Who asked you to?" and it's a good question.

Balance is the answer. Decide when to say yes and when to say no, and then do so.

Personal Pain

There are times when personal pain overtakes a parent, making it very difficult to give a child what she needs. Death, depression and divorce are all painful times when the needs of the adult can become overwhelming.

And often the things happening to the parent are also having an impact on the child, who has heightened needs as a result. One of the most difficult times can be when there is a death in the family. The parent may be overcome with grief and have no idea how to function, let alone have the energy to help the grieving child.

When someone dies other family members and friends will rally and ask, "What can I do?" Accept their help. Allow them to do things for you that will free you to help your children, or ask them to help with the children. (But try not to hand the children over too often to willing helpers; children need you in times of grief.)

IT WAS A BEAUTIFUL, SUNNY DAY. MY BROTHER GAVE THE EULOGY.

ELIZABETH SANG "CLIMB EVERY MOUNTAIN" WHICH WAS ONE OF OUR MOTHER'S FAVORITE SONGS.

ONE BY ONE, FRIENDS AND FAMILY TOLD STORIES ABOUT HER, READ POEMS THEY'D WRITTEN, SAID HOW SHE HAD INFLUENCED THEIR LIVES.

AND DAD TOLD US ALL THAT EVEN THOUGH SHE WAS GONE, HE WAS STILL THE LUCKIEST MAN ON EARTH. ... SHE HAD CHOSEN HIM AS HER PARTNER.

Divorce is a time when children are often forgotten. The parents are so busy dealing with a myriad of personal issues that they have no extra energy for the children. In fact, parents often do not recognize that divorce is equally difficult for the children.

One divorced mother who has done an excellent job of remembering her child throughout the process told me, "You need a gut-level awareness that children have needs."

There is a myth out there that children are flexible, that they can just roll with the punches, that they will have no problem adjusting. It's not true. In divorce situations children need to be recognized as people who are also suffering, who may be feeling guilty, who are experiencing loss. In a sense they are helpless bystanders: This was not their decision and it is rarely their first choice. And because they are growing and developing, they can't coast and wait until adults are ready to deal with them. They need their parents more than ever to help them understand and adjust.

IN OTHER WORDS...

Our children are precious. They need and deserve the best we can give them — the gift of quality parenting. They need parenting even when it's disruptive to our life. They need us to see what it is they need and to meet these needs. And they need our love, but do not confuse love and behavior. They are separate.

Talking about Behavior:
Kathy's Q & A

QUESTION
My seven-year-old will always find something or someone else to take the blame for his actions, even when it is obvious he is at fault. How can I get him to accept the responsibility for his actions?

ANSWER
Accepting the consequences for your mistakes or negative actions is not easy for anyone, particularly children. When you know

that he's at fault in a situation, it's best to move on to the consequences without engaging him in the argument about who or what's at fault. If your attitude is, "This happened and now it needs to be dealt with," it's harder for him to argue.

For example, if you find toys strewn all around the living room, talk about the mess. Don't deal with how they got there. "There are toys all over the floor, do you want to pick up the Lego first or the balls?" When he starts to blame someone else, simply repeat yourself: "The point is, these toys must be picked up. Do you want to pick up the Lego first, or the balls?"

Children learn more by doing, so having him pick up the toys makes the point. He's dealing with the consequences without having to accept the blame.

Using choices is also effective. He can pick up the Lego or balls first, but he's going to pick up the toys. You can also use choices when he breaks a clear rule. Instead of accusing: "You broke this rule," you can simply say, "By breaking the rule you've chosen to (suffer the consequences)."

QUESTION

My three-year-old son moved to a twin-size bed about three months ago. Ever since we set up that bed he does not sleep through the night. He gets up at least three times a night for no reason. We also have trouble putting him to bed. It takes about an hour to make him stay in his room. This gets really frustrating.

Many people have recommended that I buy a lock for his bedroom door. They say my child will quickly get the message. What do you think of this? Any suggestions?

ANSWER

First you need to consider whether your son is actually ready for bed at bedtime — maybe he just isn't tired. Try a little later. Do you have a regular bedtime ritual? Children respond best to a relaxing routine. A typical ritual involves a snack, bath and tooth brushing, then to bed and a story. Reading him a story in bed is a nice time for parent and child and allows your son to slowly settle and get ready for sleep. Unlike infants, preschoolers rarely just fall asleep, so need some help with the transition. Story time is perfect for this.

Let him have some control by allowing him to leave his bed-side light on and look at books until he's ready to fall asleep.

It is very common for children who sleep alone to get up during the night. If he has a sibling consider having them share a room. Then when he awakens at night, he's not alone. He may be having nightmares or just awakening and feeling very lonely in the dark.

Would you consider letting him come into your bed or sleep in your room when he wakes up? Some families keep a sleeping bag on the floor for lonely or frightened children.

Don't lock him in his room. Imagine if he wakes up at night and he's sick or frightened, and the very people he desperately needs have locked him away from them. What message is that giving him? It's also a safety concern. If there were an emergency, like a fire, having him in a locked room would be dangerous.

QUESTION

I am so tired of explaining everything to my ten-year-old. I always vowed I'd make sure she always understood the reasons for our decisions. But the explanations are becoming marathon sessions. What can I do?

ANSWER

You can say, "Because I said so." Parents used to use that phrase so often that the next generation determined to never use it. But sometimes, it's the correct answer. Explaining to children is a good thing. Over-explaining is not.

A common pitfall is to explain instead of taking action or following through. Your ten-year-old has probably learned that if she pushes long and hard enough for answers, she'll end up getting her own way. If she keeps you occupied talking, you'll eventually get so tired of explaining that you'll just give up. Or you won't find an acceptable explanation.

Yes, we want our children to understand the rules and expectations. But you can explain once and then get on with it. Your daughter doesn't have to agree with your reasoning, and you don't have to respond to her every question. What's more, you don't need to provide an explanation every time you ask her to do something. Your daughter has been living with you, your rules and explanations for ten years. She already knows why. Now, she needs to learn that you're going to expect her to follow the rules without the long discussion.

Chapter 7

"I LIKE ME!"
HOW TO FOSTER POSITIVE SELF-ESTEEM

"JASON," SAID MARTIN, THE FATHER OF THREE-YEAR-OLD JASON, "could you please bring me the newspaper?" Jason picked up the newspaper and brought it across the room to his dad.

"Oh, that's wonderful," Martin gushed. "You are the best helper in the world. Whenever I need any help I can call on you." But the next time Jason's dad asked a favor, Jason hesitated. He complied, but with dragging feet.

So what happened? Why did Jason feel hesitant about receiving such a positive response from his dad?

Praise often backfires. In this case the father overreacted. Even at three Jason knew that a simple "thanks, son" would have sufficed. Also, Jason now feels he has to live up to being the "best helper." What if his dad asks him to do something more difficult and he fails — then will his dad still like him?

We often use the term self-esteem, but what does it mean? For me, it's my attitude toward myself. When I judge myself as worthy, as lovable and as capable I feel I have the capacity to handle whatever life wants to hand me. It's not just liking myself; it's believing in myself and my ability to live my life no matter what the circumstances.

There is a myth about child self-esteem that suggests that if we love our kids they will know we love them no matter what we do, and this feeling of being loved builds their self-esteem. If only it were true. But while love is an essential ingredient in child self-esteem, it doesn't stand alone. I've heard many of my adult friends say of their parents, "I know she loves me but whenever I talk to her I end up feeling like such a loser."

So how do we help our children build high self-esteem?

ENCOURAGEMENT

Encouragement, rather than praise, is one way of helping children to feel good about themselves and about doing the right thing.

If you look in the dictionary you'll see that praise is defined as "an expression of warm approval or admiration" and encouragement as "giving courage, urging or promoting." In the world of parenting education we use these terms a little differently.

Praise is a type of reward, given for success that the adult defines as worthy of notice. A child might, for example, be praised for earning an A, but not for a B. And praise tends to value the person based on the accomplishment: "Selina, you're the best student in Math and English! I'm so proud of you!" Now Selina has to live up to that standard in order to get recognition from her mother. What if next term she's not "the best?"

Encouragement, by contrast, recognizes the effort or the action, not just the accomplishment. Children need recognition beyond their successes. Childhood is a time of trial and error, and in order to have the strength to try again and again after a failure, a child needs to know that his struggle is being acknowledged. In the example above, Selina would probably be happier with a comment like: "That's great, Selina. You worked very hard for those marks." Now Selina knows it's important to try to *do* her best,

Praise and Encouragement: What's the Difference?

PRAISE

- Is ego oriented: "You are so wonderful."

- Is given for a deed well done: "That's great — 100% in Math again!"

- Emphasizes the child: "You're the best hitter on the team."

- Develops dependence: the child becomes reluctant to do anything without praise and recognition.

- Fosters anxiety: if you don't get praise, you must be doing something wrong.

- Fosters fear of failure: the child wonders if he will be able to "measure up" to the same standard next time.

- Is patronizing, condescending: "You did a fantastic job!" The child may not feel that it was a good job.

ENCOURAGEMENT

- Fosters realistic self-worth: "You were really kind to that little girl."

- Is given for trying, even if the result was failure: "What a great effort."

- Emphasizes the action: "Your home run helped the team win the game."

- Develops independence: by teaching the child to find satisfaction within himself.

- Fosters self-confidence: the child realizes his contribution is valued.

- Presents mistakes as a form of growth. "So you blew it that time. Let's see what we can learn for next time."

- Shares the feeling of the parent, but allows the child to have a different feeling: "I appreciate the help you gave me."

- Encouragement is based on trust, confidence and hope.

but not to *be* the best. It's her hard work that is valued, not her ranking against other children. As long as she is trying, her parents will acknowledge the effort given. She doesn't need to reach a particular goal to get her parents' approval.

Praise is an attempt to motivate children with external rewards. Sometimes the rewards are tangible, as when a parent pays a child for high marks. Sometimes they are verbal: "I am so proud of you!" says Selina's mom. When parents use this kind of praise to motivate children, they often only recognize their accomplishments when they reach a pre-determined target, such as the A on the test.

Encouragement is an attempt to motivate the child through internal means. By describing the child's behavior, it teaches her to evaluate and value her own efforts: She eventually does it for her own satisfaction, not for a pat on the head from someone else. You can encourage your child by saying: "You worked hard on that." "It took courage to try out for the play, even if you didn't get the part." "Your help made those dishes go a lot faster. Thanks." Remember, in the long term you want your child to work hard and do what's right for her own self-respect, not just to please you!

TRUST

Children are dependent on their parents, so they need to know that they can trust the people who are caring for them. Without the feeling of safety that comes from trusting the primary people in their lives, children become insecure. When they don't know what to trust, they can't relax and simply mature, let alone develop a positive image of themselves.

We aren't intentionally dishonest but certainly we sometimes avoid the truth with our children. Public health nurses in my workshops have told me that they would like to set aside a very special corner in hell for parents who bring children into the clinic for a vaccination and say to the nurse, "I told him he didn't have to have a shot today because I didn't want him to be upset and I know you can handle it."

We build trust and self-esteem with our children when we let them know what to expect and give them the message that we know they can cope with difficult experiences. "We're going to the clinic today because it's time for your booster shot. The nurse will have a needle to put in your arm and it will prick a little and maybe sting a bit for a minute, and it may also be sore and itchy for the rest of the day. But I know you can handle it." What a strong positive self-esteem message. If a child cries when he gets his shot, remember that crying is a method of coping, not failure. So let him know that crying is perfectly acceptable, he doesn't need to try to avoid tears.

CHALLENGE AND SUPPORT

Six-year-old Laurie is learning how to ride her new bike. She has training wheels on the back and her father is holding the seat, helping her maintain her balance as she learns this new skill. It takes time, it takes practice and it will probably involve a couple of tumbles off the bike. But the work finally pays off when she heads off on her own. The smile on her face lights up the whole neighborhood. It was hard work, it was worth it and she feels terrific about herself.

Nine-year-old Blair is working on a science project for school. He disappears into his room and shows up 20 minutes later saying that he's finished. His stepmother, Dana, wonders how that can be possible and asks if she can see the finished product. He proudly shows her a quick drawing of the solar system. It's not to scale nor is it very detailed. She makes no comment but her husband is extremely complimentary. Later Dana asks her husband how he can respond so positively to such a mediocre piece of work. "Blair's mother and I are committed to appreciating everything he does so that he will develop high self-esteem. We expect that the more we applaud his work the better he will feel."

It doesn't work that way. Children know when they have worked hard and when they haven't. When Blair is lauded for any minuscule attempt at a project, he learns that mediocre is good enough. Moreover, he may well think his dad believes that's the best he can do.

We need to encourage our children as they struggle to reach a goal, whether it is bike riding or a science project. But we also need to challenge them to keep trying until they have achieved their best. Note that the operative word is *their* best. We should encourage kids to reach their own potential, whatever that is.

Hard work and struggle lead to success that develops self-esteem.

NO MAN IS AN ISLAND

Encouragement will motivate children to behave in ways that are appropriate and socially acceptable. But they can't instinctively know what is correct. It's up to parents to introduce children to the concept of social order. No man is an island. Our behavior impacts on all those around us. Children need to learn to consider the rights and needs of others. That's building character.

Doing the right thing involves more than a list of rules and expectations. Children are masters at interpreting rules to meet their own needs.

Karen asked her ten-year-old son, Johnny, to take out the garbage. She was thrilled when his response was, "Sure." Three hours later the truck passed but their garbage was still on the porch. Then, she wasn't so happy.

"Johnny, I thought you said you'd take out the garbage. Well, it's still here and the truck has passed. Why can't you do what I ask you?"

"You didn't say when," was the calm reply.

Teaching children to think beyond the literal translation of rules is part of the task of helping them build character. It's learning how to assess a situation and do what needs to be done or avoid behavior that might hurt someone. It's developmentally appropriate for a ten-year-old to respond as Johnny did. Karen needs to learn to give more exact instructions. As he ages, she will add information to help him to think through his responsibilities. "The garbage truck will be here by noon and we'd like the garbage to be out for pick-up." Now it's not just a chore. Johnny is responsible for saving the family from the inconvenience and smell of garbage which has to be kept around for another week.

Children who learn to consider the big picture, the needs of the situation and the group, are the ones we simply call nice. These are people who tend to be welcomed by others, which is in itself a great self-esteem booster.

IN OTHER WORDS...

High self-esteem is not simply given to kids. It is earned by effort. Encouragement is the tool toward success. We challenge children to set realistic goals and encourage them as they work hard to reach their goals. Our confidence in their ability to work hard to achieve their best motivates them to stick to the task at hand.

Children's positive self-esteem comes from our encouragement and trust and from their own eventual success.

Talking about Behavior
Kathy's Q & A

QUESTION

Reports cards were handed out last week in my daughter's grade two class, and she discovered that her friend gets rewarded with money and small gifts for every good mark she receives. My daughter is a good student, and I tell her so with lots of hugs and thumbs up when she does well, but it has never occurred to me to reward her with gifts or money. At first I thought perhaps this other parent was setting herself up for doling out years of more and more expensive gifts — but then I started to wonder. If you keep it simple, maybe it isn't such a bad idea. What do you think?

ANSWER

Going to school and doing the best they can is a task of childhood. Doing her best should not require bribes of gifts and money. You're doing the right thing by acknowledging your daughter's success and I hope you will continue even if she doesn't always get top marks. As long as she's working hard and doing her best, that's what counts.

Often when kids receive rewards for marks they end up working for the reward, not for the self-satisfaction that comes from doing a good job. They need to get something every time they succeed and it can evolve into a "What's in it for me?" mentality.

And the requests for reward can definitely accelerate as the child ages. What will it take to have her graduate high school? A car?

Stick with your style; it's best for your daughter.

QUESTION

My three-year-old daughter, Tansy, is my best friend. I love to do things with her. How can I maintain this relationship?

ANSWER

I'm so pleased that you enjoy being with Tansy. Having fun with your kids can make the whole parenting job so much easier.

However, she needs you to be her parent, not her best friend. As a parent you have a responsibility to set the limits, define expectations, love unconditionally and so on. These are not compatible with being best friends.

She can have lots of friends throughout her life, but only one Mom. It's a special and wonderful relationship. Enjoy that.

Being her mom, you can have fun with her, play together, laugh, joke, tell stories, go to movies and out to dinner. And it will feel just like a friendship. Parents should be friendly with their kids and enjoy spending time with them. But kids need to develop friendships with their peers. And they need you to be there to parent.

When you are your daughter's best friend it can be difficult to be the disciplinarian or advisor. Sometimes when parents are best friends to their children, the kids don't spend time with their peers and end up lonely.

Continue to spend time with Tansy and have fun with her. Just remember you, and only you, are her mom.

QUESTION

I'm going to be sending my daughter Cheryl to preschool in the fall. I've been hearing a lot about co-operative preschools. Is this a good choice and if so, why?

ANSWER

I'm a great supporter of co-operative preschools because they are good for both preschoolers and their parents.

I can remember the days when my friends and I talked about our young children, sharing our stories of toilet training, the first day of school and birthday parties. That was over 20 years ago. Now we talk about weddings, grandchildren and our children's careers. Different stories, but the same friends. And I met many of them through my children's co-operative preschool.

Busy parents often find the concept of participating in their child's preschool to be overwhelming and don't even consider the option. Let me talk to you about the benefits.

Research shows that parent involvement is a major factor in child success. In my experience parents who start participating with their children at the preschool or daycare level continue to do so through elementary and high school.

There are demands made on your time, but the level of participation can be geared to suit your schedule. You may choose to participate in the administration of the school by sitting on the board of directors or a committee. You can be in the class with your child once or twice a month. Or you can receive the newsletter and take advantage of evening social events with other parents.

The children are engaged in a quality program with a qualified teacher. Teachers who choose a co-operative school bring an appreciation for the role of parents into the school situation. They are not only committed to quality early childhood education, they are committed to partnering with parents to make the experience for all parties the best it can be.

Being involved in your child's education benefits both you and your child. It's the very demands of participation that make the experience so worthwhile. You will meet other parents who share many of your values about the importance of quality parenting, learn more about child-raising and work with like-minded and usually nice people toward joint goals. And you will make friends for life.

QUESTION

My ten-year-old son still likes to come and sleep in our room in the middle of the night. He doesn't come in our bed but has a foamy and blanket and sleeps on the floor at the end of the bed. He's an only child and is fearful someone will break into our home.

Although he's nervous at night, he is outgoing and confident in all other situations.

I've been telling him it's time for him to stay in his own room but he gets very upset. What is better for his self-esteem — letting him come in until he outgrows his fear or give him the big push and insist he sleep in his own room?

ANSWER

I'd let him come and sleep in your room. It's not causing you any problems and is certainly making him feel more comfortable.

He'll make the decision about when he's ready to be on his own. Meanwhile, he needs your presence at night. After all, many adults say that when their spouse is away they feel nervous.

It's likely that he's confident and outgoing in other situations because he's getting the support he needs at night. If he's forced to stay alone in the dark when he's nervous he's not going to feel confident and secure. But the fact that you're there for him when he needs it counts for a lot.

Chapter 8

WHAT'S THE MAGIC WORD?
WHY MANNERS MATTER

YOU'RE VISITING A FRIEND. YOU RING THE DOORBELL. YOU HEAR yells as children tumble over each other as they race to the door, screaming, "I'll get it, I'll get it!" The door opens and the children stop dead in their tracks and stare at you. They then turn tail and run, yelling, "Mom, Mom, there's someone at the door." Mother arrives red-faced, and apologizes for her children's behavior. "You know how kids are," she says. You understand, because you've been there too.

In recent years I've sensed a growing desire for a return to civility, politeness and manners. Is it a reaction to the Me Generation and the drive for individual freedom that has marked the last decade? Whatever it is, our society's rebirth of interest in good manners is a trend I thoroughly enjoy. When you look at your long-term hopes for your kids, isn't it going to be necessary for them to have good manners to meet some of these goals?

Friends, relatives, teachers, neighbors and potential employers all judge our children by their manners. As parents we have a major role to play in helping them develop these important social graces.

MANNERS IN PUBLIC

There's nothing like going out in public to shine a spotlight on children's manners. Suddenly, manners matter.

"Jeremy, would you like a drink of juice?"

"Yes."

The parent prompts, "Yes what, Jeremy?"

"Huh?"

"What's the magic word, Jeremy?"

"Oh, yes please."

"Here's some juice, Jeremy."

The child reaches for the juice and starts to drink.

"What do you say, Jeremy?"

No answer from the child, who is busy drinking.

"Say thank you, Jeremy."

"Thanks."

The parent looks over with the resigned look of someone who goes through this on every visit. In social situations parents become painfully aware of their children's lack of manners, and these embarrassments often drive them to do something about it.

There are major problems with the "what's the magic word?" scenario, particularly when it goes well beyond a gentle reminder and becomes a routine for both parent and child. Generally what's being taught (and learned) is that when it's important or appropriate to say please or thank you, the parent will give a prompt. The other side of that coin is that saying please isn't always important, because Mom and Dad don't insist on it as a matter of routine.

When you expect good manners, children are more likely to meet the expectations. If they hear you say, "I can't take her any-where" or "I wish he would say please but..." they're learning that their parents expect them to be impolite.

Many parents have told me that basic good manners are not particularly difficult for children to master. Most children are eager to learn how to behave in ways that are respectful of other people. But good manners and social skills are not genetic. They will not suddenly emerge when the child reaches a certain age. They have to be modeled and taught.

OUR CHILDREN WILL DO WHAT WE DO

As adults in close relationships with our spouses we tend, over time, to get a bit casual in the manners department. When we have children we're much too busy dealing with every variety of infant crisis to pay proper attention to how we're treating each other.

Suddenly our toddler becomes a preschooler and starts to interact with his world, based on what he has seen and heard at home. Unlike adults, he can't suddenly switch into good manners mode when the situation calls for it, because he lacks that experience.

The only sure way to raise polite, socially skilled children is to expect good manners in all cases, not just in front of company. Most parents find that introducing manners when children are young and modeling them at home every day is a sure-fire way to get the job done.

A mother tells of a visit to a neighbor for a barbecue. Four-year-old Riley was on his best behavior, and when he was asked if he'd like a second hot dog he answered carefully and oh-so-politely, "No, thank you. I don't like the burned kind." Now that's pretty good for four, and the neighbor appreciated the manners if not the message!

An essential (and easily forgotten) part of modeling good manners is being polite and considerate to our kids and their friends.

A father was taking a group photo at a family picnic. Everyone smiled gamely for a full 30 seconds, but Dad still hadn't taken the picture.

"Take the picture, already. The food's getting cold," someone finally said.

Dad replied: "I'm waiting for my daughter Sheila to stop trying out that goofy smile of hers." Sheila, a self-conscious 13-year-old, was mortified in front of her relatives. She fought back her tears and was sullen for the rest of the event.

Parents and other adults need to consider the feelings and needs of children. If adults talk about them when they're in the room, ignore them while carrying on long, boring conversations, or forget to plan for their needs on a visit, you can be sure they'll behave poorly.

A neighborhood open house was just ending and a mother and child were leaving. The host suddenly remembered something she wanted to discuss and held up the mother well beyond the limit of the child's patience.

Mom dealt with the situation as best she could by keeping a hand on the child's shoulder and patting her hair to show she wasn't entirely ignored. She soon ended the conversation with "I'll call you tomorrow to talk about that," and headed down the sidewalk waving a cheery goodbye. Nice save.

CHILDREN NEED TO BE TAUGHT

As part of the teaching, plan some practice sessions. These can include answering the door and the phone, having adult guests in your home, visiting relatives and other common situations.

If your children have poor table manners, set aside a night as a chance to learn. Again, without lecturing or sarcasm, coach the children through the process. Then, put the table manners into practice in your own home, with everyone participating. Children who have learned these skills are more comfortable with adults. It starts with parents who engage them in conversation at the table, in the car and sitting in the living room. The key word here is conversation, not lecture.

Children should also be taught to take responsibility for the well-being of visiting children. They can show them where to hang up their coats, introduce them to their parents, other adults and each other, offer drinks, arrange games and advise them of house rules.

SHY AND EXCITABLE KIDS

In some cases our expectations can outstrip a child's ability to cope. Some children are painfully shy, others are prone to anxiety attacks in certain situations and others are very active. Parents need to recognize these realities and develop strategies for their children where they can achieve some success.

Often, a shy child can handle introductions better if he's holding a parent's hand. An excitable child might be able to say hi and chat for a minute if she knows she can soon escape to the back yard and burn off some steam. You know your child; work within his or her realistic capabilities.

Rehearse Your First Visit

One good way to make young children comfortable in a new social situation is to practice it. Make it fun, but instructive. If you're planning an afternoon visit with Uncle Harold and Aunt Betty, set the scene.

Sit down with the children and explain what's likely to happen. You'll go to their door and ring the bell. They'll invite you in, lead you to the living room, and offer you a choice of things to drink.

In the rehearsal, Mom can wear a sign around her neck saying Aunt Betty, Dad wears the Uncle Harold sign and the kids are sent outside to ring the doorbell.

The door opens and Aunt Betty says, "Hello, good to see you, please come in."

The children are prompted to say "Hello, Aunt Betty."

Uncle Harold appears and says, "How are you two?"

Children: "Fine, Uncle Harold."

In the living room Aunt Betty says "Would you like a drink? I have water, juice or a Coke, if your mom will let you have one."

"I'd like a Coke, please."

And, of course, "Thank you."

A scene like this takes only a few minutes to act out, even if you run through it a second or third time. It will help prepare the children for the visit and make them feel less apprehensive.

At a relatively young age children should be able to make good eye contact with adults and answer questions about their age, their grade in school, what sports they play, and so on. "What's your teacher like?" or "What's your favorite subject?" are Aunt/Uncle/Grandma-type questions, but ones a six-year-old may have never been asked. When children are not adequately prepared for such questions they may simply freeze and shrug, so a little coaching is in order. A few rehearsed answers could come in very useful, and will represent the beginnings of conversation for a young child.

Children can also be coached to ask, after an appropriate interval, "May I leave the table now?" or "Can we go outside and play?" And a "Thank you" when permission is granted.

SOME BASIC SOCIAL GRACES ALL KIDS CAN MASTER

So we want our kids to be polite, to have the social graces they need to succeed in life. Whatever you decided you want for your kids when they turn 18, the reality is that without social graces they're unlikely to be successful.

But what should they know and when? They can master more social skills than you imagine.

A preschooler should be able play quietly during a social event for a short time, and by the time she's in school be able to sit at the table and eat and visit for about 20 minutes. By age six she can take the coat of a visitor and engage in a short conversation. An eight-year-old can shake hands and give good eye contact when meeting a new person and a teenager can be expected to engage in social chitchat with anyone for a short time.

School-aged children can be taught to say a word of thanks after receiving a gift or a meal which includes a comment such as, "That was a great dinner."

In saying goodbye after a visit it's reasonable to expect kids to say thanks (for dinner, a swim in the pool or whatever) and the children of the host should add "Bye, thanks for coming."

Please and thank you

One Hallowe'en I went to our door to drop some goodies into the bags of an eager band of ghosts and goblins. As the last little four-year-old turned and tripped down the steps, I couldn't fail to notice the sign a thoughtful parent had taped to her goblin's back. It said Thank You.

When children are just learning to speak, we're usually delighted when they learn new words. Instead of pointing, the young child says "milk" and as parents we count this as progress. But as these same patterns continue into preschool age, parents suddenly discover they've forgotten to introduce the concept of please and thank you.

If children are to learn to use please and thank you it must be typical family behavior. But it won't work unless the parents use please and thank you with each other as well as with the children. Reminding is not a good teaching tool. It's much more effective to spell out the expectation, then refuse to listen until the orders stop and polite requests begin.

Answering the telephone and the door

A very young child cannot be expected to take a complicated telephone message. But once a child can write, taking a simple message is a reasonable expectation.

We need to teach our children how to answer the phone. Practice with them and be patient. Let them speak to people they know for a few minutes. It will satisfy their curiosity about the phone and will teach them how to use it properly. If a child is too young to answer the telephone appropriately, she should be discouraged from answering it at all.

Children also need to be taught how to answer the door, how to show known or expected guests into the home, and how to respond to simple social comments. The best way to teach these skills is to rehearse them with the child. This also allows you to rehearse those situations where the child should not open the door or should not answer questions.

Shaking hands

This is becoming a lost art. Today, both boys and girls need to learn how. A good handshake creates a positive first impression.

If we teach our children to shake hands, we will give them the ability to greet people appropriately, and to politely avoid hugging people whom they do not wish to hug. A good, firm handshake will be a valuable asset for our children as they grow older and need to assert themselves.

(Not) whispering

Whispering is rude. Children often whisper to adults in public. The rationale is that the child is not disrupting the conversation, but whispering can be more disruptive than a louder interruption. As well, a whisper leaves the impression a secret is being shared and that makes people feel uncomfortable. Children can learn to wait for a break, excuse themselves and make the request, or ask their parent to come away if they need to speak privately.

Consideration for others

Interrupting, running through the middle of a conversational grouping, yelling nearby, or watching television in a room where there is also conversation are other common behaviors that don't endear children to visiting adults. Children can be taught that such behaviors are inappropriate.

And one for the adults: Make room for kids

Children who wish to join a conversation can do so in all the ways a polite adult accomplishes the same goal. However, the adults need to be alert to a child who wants to join in the conversation, and make room for him to break in with his comment.

BE PREPARED: KIDS' SOCIAL CHALLENGES

Children need our help in certain social situations. Adults don't always realize that these special occasions can be hard for children to cope with.

Children's birthday parties

We've all watched "the big rip" — the birthday girl or boy madly unwrapping a pile of gifts, barely taking time to breathe. In the excitement of it all she has no idea what the gift was or who brought it.

One woman I know offers her children one gift at a time, comments on each gift and repeats who it's from. She has coached her daughter to say a sincere thank you. You can model the words: "Look Jennifer, Jill got you a purple T-shirt with yellow butterflies. Butterflies are your favorite!" Jennifer may follow this with a "Yeah, thanks Jill."

Her friend Jill is very excited about the gift she selected and needs some recognition. Young children bringing gifts are almost as excited as the birthday child. They want the recipient to like the gift they chose. We can teach our children to express their appreciation.

It happens that children get gifts they don't like or something they already have. We all deal with this as adults, but in their disappointment children can easily say the wrong (but honest) thing. It would be useful to prepare your child for this eventuality by explaining that people choose gifts because they want to please the recipient. The child can thank them publicly for their thoughtfulness and generosity so as not to hurt their feelings. Later on you can help arrange to exchange the gift if that's appropriate.

Family visits

Once children are overtired or have eaten too much, particularly if they're on a sugar high from candy, it's unrealistic to expect them to behave well. But with some planning it's possible to have fun at all these events, to relax the rules and schedules a bit and still maintain some decorum.

Your child may have no idea what to expect so prepare her before the event by telling her what will happen, and lay out your expectations. Manage the environment: take a look at the number of people, the amount of space and the activity needs of your child. A birthday party can be managed by reducing the guest list, by having the party outdoors, by planning fun activities, and by keeping it short. Reunions can take place near or in parks, around swimming pools or in homes big enough to accommodate the play needs of the children.

Plan for some large-muscle play — running, jumping, a quick trip to a neighborhood park or school ground to play on climbing bars. Kids need some energetic play in their day, particularly if they're also expected to play quietly for long periods during a visit.

Try to maintain meal and sleep routines. Children's behavior tends to deteriorate when their body clock is out of whack.

Pay attention: know where your child is and monitor his ability to cope with the excitement. Sometimes quietly removing your child on some pretext for ten minutes can defuse a situation. Engaging the children in a story or other quiet activity may calm down the whole group.

If you know there won't be other kids for your child to play with, bring along some toys or games. Make an effort to ease him into the adult conversation if he wants to say something.

When it's time to leave, give your child some notice, then say your goodbyes and leave.

Formal dinners

Depending on your family style, birthdays for adult relatives, family celebrations, or Thanksgiving dinners may be more formal in terms of the table setting, food and dress.

Parents can first suggest certain modifications that will make their children more comfortable. Young children need to eat on time. A meal served late can be a disaster. An early chat with the hostess can be useful in determining the timing, and help you plan a snack and other activities to keep your child busy. Make sure that the chair is high enough and at least some dishes are appropriate to the age of the child. Within these kinds of guidelines, children can learn about a more formal type of eating and have fun.

Young children cannot be expected to sit quietly at the table for long periods. One mother I spoke with allows her youngest to leave the table and play once he's finished his main course. Then, he rejoins the family for dessert. Cutting the sitting in two makes it an enjoyable meal for children and adults alike.

Places of worship

Going to church, to weddings and to funerals call for different protocols. Children are expected to dress appropriately, sit still and be quiet. When children are young it's a good idea to sit near the back so you can slip outside with a fussy or fidgety toddler. For older children, again, you can prepare them at home beforehand by practicing.

A parent can make a church visit or wedding ceremony a bit of an adventure by quietly explaining to the child the layout of the church, what's going to happen next, and who all the people are before the service begins. This will help the child understand and appreciate the ceremony, and will also occupy him and help him feel more comfortable in that ten minutes before the action starts.

Funerals are much more difficult. Young children particularly have not had much experience with the concept of death. They'll need some explanation appropriate to their age. They'll also need to know that most of the people there will be sad and many adults will cry.

The mourners don't need to wear black these days, but children should dress in subdued and simple clothing. There is no need to buy very expensive formal clothes for growing children, but they can wear something more formal than play clothes.

Restaurants

Deciding that you won't take Jonah to a restaurant until he's 25 years old is not the answer. What's needed is a bit of planning, and coaching about how restaurants work.

Go to a restaurant when Jonah is hungry but before starvation is setting in. When the server arrives ask for a glass of milk and some crackers. This will stave off starvation-induced tantrums while you order your meal.

Rehearse Telephone Calls

Here's a basic script to help kids learn to answer the phone:

It's not a good idea to teach children to answer with their name. Leave that for the office. A simple "Hello" does just fine.

Caller: "May I speak to your mother/father/Mary?"

(If home) "Yes, just a minute please."

Or (If not home) "I'm sorry, she can't come to the phone right now. Who's calling please?"

(Get a name, if not a relative or neighbor known to the child.)

"Does she have your number?" (or, "Please wait, I'll get a pencil and write it down.")

"I'll give her the message. Thanks for calling. Goodbye."

Children also need to know how to call a friend:

"Hello, could I please speak to Jane?"

(Or, if she recognizes the voice on the phone she could identify yourself) "Hello, Mrs. Smith, this is Mary. Could I please speak to Jane?"

(If not home) "Could you have her call me? She has my number. Thank you."

Once the meal is ordered, it is time to explore. Take him for a walk around the building or to the washroom. Washrooms fascinate children and it's an acceptable way to fill in time until the food arrives. If dessert is planned, order it while the children are still eating, to be delivered right after the main course. Ask for the bill at the same time. If you're lucky, you can get in a few sips of post-meal coffee while your child is busy with dessert.

When you are in a restaurant with children, accord them the same consideration you would an adult. Include them in the conversation and listen to their comments and stories. Don't even think about having a serious adult conversation over the meal! If you ignore them, your children will quickly get bored and will make your life miserable.

TEACHING TACT

Tact is another skill children need to learn. It starts, as with all social skills, with modeling. When your sister gives you a sweater that is truly ugly, how do you respond? If you put the feelings and needs of your sister first, your children will see that and find it easier to do the same when they receive a dorky shirt from Great Aunt Mabel.

When you hear your children in the other room being rude and inconsiderate toward others, you can teach them better ways of speaking. If they have guests, wait until you're alone with them. It's not necessary to become angry or disgusted. They were just saying how they feel. "Agnes, I heard you tell Cheryl that she's too fat to wear a short skirt. That may be true, but it's not nice to say anything. You hurt her feelings."

"But, Mom, you've always told me to be honest."

"That's true. But you could be honest without hurting her feelings. Maybe you could just say that you love that color on her."

These skills will not only help our children to become more considerate and kind. They will ease their path as they become known as nice, co-operative and helpful people, people of good character.

IN OTHER WORDS ...

The keys to teaching manners are modeling, expectations and teaching. When parents model good manners, children will see and imitate.

Give your children the gift of graciousness. A child who is polite, who can handle social situations, meet new people and enjoy a good conversation has a gift from you that will last a lifetime.

Talking about Behavior
Kathy's Q & A

QUESTION

My ten-year-old daughter, Carolyn, receives gifts from out-of-town relatives on birthdays and at Christmas. I try to get her to write thank-you letters, but it's like pulling teeth. What should I do?

ANSWER

Good manners include a gracious acceptance of gifts. Thank-you letters are increasingly rare but, I believe, very important. I'd suggest that you schedule a time when all the members of the household write their letters. If you sit down with your children it becomes a family event and easier for everyone. Don't engage in any arguments. Simply state that you expect her to write. Say something like, "It's now letter-writing time. I have a list of the people who sent gifts and what they sent, so let's get to it."

You can help her by suggesting things she might talk about. Out-of-town relatives are interested in all aspects of her life so talking about the school party or a planned skating outing with friends will be a hit. If you have pictures of your daughter with the gift it's a real bonus to include them or if she received money she can tell them what she's planning on buying. In some cases an email or phone call works well but I do have a bias that says taking the time and effort to write a letter and post it is special.

QUESTION

I have two children, six and eight. They always forget to say please and thank you. It seems like I spend all day reminding them. When will they remember on their own?

ANSWER

When your children have a reason to remember they'll do so. Right now they only have to say please and thank you after you tell them to, so they don't have to think of it on their own.

Let them know that you're finished reminding them. Tell them that when they ask for something politely you'll hear them. Then when they run in and say; "Mom, can I have a cookie?" ignore them. Don't remind about the new rule. Just stay silent and continue with whatever you were doing.

They're old enough to figure it out. If you stick to your plan they will soon incorporate please and thank you into all their requests.

Of course, it's also important that you speak politely to them when making requests.

QUESTION

I'm concerned about my 27-month old daughter and my friend's son. He's only 17 months but when they play together he's very aggressive. When she is playing with a toy, he comes by and grabs it from her. If she's riding a toy, he will come along and push her off. She turns into the passive one and relinquishes the toy. What should we do? I'm starting to feel sorry for my daughter.

ANSWER

First, talk to your friend. The next time it happens you might turn to her and say, "Do you think we could work together to help the kids share their toys?" However, you also have to keep in mind that these are very young children, especially the boy. Children at this young age can be extremely possessive. At 17 months he's just getting a sense of himself as a person and his toys as his. When he grabs it is simply that he can only understand that he wants that toy. He has no sense of what he's doing to her. Therefore, it will take adult intervention to help them learn how to change their responses.

So, when he grabs a toy from your daughter, his mother or you can calmly take it from him and say, "It's not nice to grab." You hand it back to your daughter who has also heard your remark.

Then, you might suggest to your daughter that it's the little boy's turn and allow her to hand it to him nicely. You are now teaching them the manners they need in order to socialize with other people.

When the little boy does something rough (like push your daughter off a riding toy) his mother can scoop him up and say, "It's not nice to hurt other people."

You don't want to make the mistake of having long explanatory discussions with these children. They are both too young.

A lot of the problems may subside as they each become more verbal.

QUESTION

My seven-year-old son was angry with me today. Usually he would just stomp off and call me a meanie. Today he called me much worse. I couldn't believe the words that were coming out of his mouth. What can I do?

ANSWER

Why do our kids use those words? You know, the ones that suddenly pop out of their mouths and make us blush.

Kids are natural mimics and we love it when they repeat all the words we use. As our little one points to the sky and says clouds or airplane we beam with pleasure. But one day the word that comes out of that sweet innocent mouth is not so fine. How could this happen?

Simple — he heard it and now he's repeating it. Just like clouds or airplane, he was interested in this new and interesting word.

First, you may need to clean up your own language. He listens to you most of all. Of course, you're not the only person he listens to and he may very well have picked up his new colorful language at school or at his soccer game. But you are the primary model for what is appropriate.

Let your son know in a matter-of-fact way that certain words are just not okay. Then get busy teaching him other new and exciting words and he may just forget that lovely curse word. This is particularly true if you don't react in an interesting fashion. If he persists in wanting to swear, make up a nonsense word instead and go with that.

Children are really interested in language, so define the words that your son is using in language he can understand. So you can say: "That's a crude and nasty way to talk about adults hugging and kissing and making love. Is that what you meant?" When he looks appalled, you offer an alternative. "I think you want to say that you're just furious that I won't let you do what you want."

Remember kids love to learn new words and to get our attention. So pay attention to the acceptable language!

Chapter 9

I WANT IT NOW!
WHEN LESS IS MORE

MARIE REALLY LOOKS FRAZZLED: HER HAIR FLYING ALL OVER THE place, her shirt only partly tucked into her jeans and her face set in an unhappy frown.

It's a typical Saturday for this mother of two school-aged kids. Up at the crack of dawn to take Becky off to swimming and Jasmine to soccer. Back to swimming to watch her daughter race, then the two of them rush off to catch the end of her sister's soccer game.

After a drive-through lunch eaten in the car, they head to the mall as Jasmine needs new jeans and Becky must have the latest runners.

Then it's drama class (Becky) and dance (Jasmine). They get home in the late afternoon just as four friends arrive for a sleepover. Mom prepares dinner for the six girls, cleans up and takes them to the video store to choose their movies.

The evening is taken up with preparing an unending supply of snacks for the girls and helping them get organized for the night — a night that doesn't include sleeping as far as the excited kids are concerned. At two in the morning, Marie finally lays down a lights-out and quiet law. Sunday is not much different.

Why does she do this every weekend? She does it, she would say, because she's a good mother. The kids are involved in a range of activities, they need stuff all the time and they need to be with their friends. And it's up to the parents to make it all happen, now.

But why? Why does everything have to happen *now*? And do the kids need — or even benefit from — all this activity each and every weekend? Sometimes it's even unclear whose idea it is that the kids participate in these activities. What is clear is that too many kids are missing down time. I think of the image of the tow-headed youngster lying in the grass, with a piece of straw sticking out of his mouth as he lazily contemplates the shapes of the clouds. No child needs to be scheduled every night of the week and most of the weekend. Every child (and adult for that matter) needs some time to relax, to simply be.

Today more than ever before, we see ourselves reflected in the successes of our children. Maybe it's because we have fewer children or because many of us wait so long before becoming parents. Maybe it's the faster pace of life in general. In past generations parents also saw themselves reflected in their children, but tended to think in terms of them as adults: my son the doctor, my daughter the lawyer. Now it starts earlier — my pre-schooler is the top swimmer in her class or my eight-year-old the top scorer on her team. Parents want their child to have every advantage, so he will get into the best post-secondary school or become a professional athlete. But it's also nice to be the parent of the great ten-year-old gymnast.

INSTANT TECHNOLOGY, INSTANT GRATIFICATION?

Email brings instant answers, the Internet brings instant information. There's no need to wait for the mail service or go to the library to research a question. It's all there, right now.

So there's a developing culture that says you shouldn't have to wait for anything. And as culture touches all aspects of our lives, we end up looking to our kids for instant reinforcement of the job we're doing.

But that's at odds with child development. Children grow slowly, develop skills as a process and cause their parents' patience to run thin as they push at the limits. If we slow down and enjoy and respect their process and their pace, raising kids is a richly rewarding experience. But when we expect instant gratification, it's hard on us and on our kids.

Children, too, need to learn to how to wait.

Andrea and Janelle were talking about an upcoming party, planned in two weeks for the preschool. Janelle said her kids were all excited and could hardly wait. Andrea said that she hadn't told her kids about it. She said she'd tell them on the morning of the party. She couldn't stand being with them when they were excited with the anticipation of an upcoming event. She also said that she didn't want them to be disappointed if they got sick and had to miss it.

It seems to make sense, but Andrea's strategy actually doesn't help her kids grow and develop. For them, the time lag between anticipating the party and experiencing it is negligible. So how can they learn to plan for something, to save for something, to wait? It's important for children to know that often we have to work for something we want or wait for it. It's equally valuable for them to occasionally experience the disappointment of waking up with a sore throat and fever on party day and have to miss the activity. That's life.

A SENSE OF ENTITLEMENT

Children have a right to expect that they will grow up with love, safety and security. I see this (with apologies to Jean-Luc Picard of the Starship *Enterprise*) as The Prime Directive of Parenting. But that doesn't mean having a perfect life or getting everything you want when you want it. It doesn't even mean *ever* getting everything you want.

We need to teach children to recognize their responsibility to the family and to the community. They will be cared for, as will the rest of the family. Part of that responsibility is learning that none of us gets what we want or even need immediately, every time. Someone else may have a greater need. Sometimes that's as simple as waiting a few minutes to get your attention while you change the baby.

In our busy lives we feel a strong sense of guilt when we're too busy at work or home to give the kids all the time we'd like. In Chapter Six we spoke about the myth of quality time. Kids need to know that if they really need us we'll be there, that we're thinking of them and that they are our priority. That's not the same as being entitled to whatever you want when you want it. Wants and needs are different.

I need to eat every day in order to stay healthy. I want to go out to a fancy restaurant for dinner, but I don't *need* to go to the restaurant in order to eat or stay healthy.

You can never give children too much love. But you *can* give them too much: too much stuff, too much service, too much instant gratification. "Too much" gives the kids the message that they should have what they want, when they want it. Is this a goal you have for your child? Did you plan that when he's 18 he'll believe he is entitled to anything he wants, can have everything at once and that his parents will always give it to him? Somehow I doubt it.

LETTING THEM GO

Our children need to be loved, safe and secure. Security comes when they know we're there for them. We're their greatest fans and loudest cheerleaders. Safety comes when we arm them with the skill and knowledge to make the journey to independence.

It's interesting that while we are quick — maybe too quick — to give our children things, we find it difficult to give them the independence they both crave and need. When we overprotect our children we do them no favors. When we give them independence, whether that be increased responsibility or privileges as they mature, we arm them for the future.

It's a scary process to let them go, but we must. We start by letting them fall on their well-padded bottoms as they learn to walk. We create a safe environment so they won't hit sharp table corners or fall downstairs, and then we let them practice walking.

We let them make choices, easy ones at first. "It's cold today — do you want to wear your green sweater or the brown one?"

We teach them how to get to school on their own. I live in a big city and I remember the first time my daughter was going downtown by bus with a friend. It was a Saturday afternoon, she was a responsible kid and she was ready. But I panicked and said, "I'm not sure I'm ready for this!" Her calm answer was, "Mom, you're not often ready when I do something new — but you catch up real fast."

IN OTHER WORDS...

We can give our children a great gift when we permit them to wait. Whether it's taking swimming this term and pottery next rather than both at once, or waiting until Christmas for the new bike, they learn valuable lessons. They learn to make choices and to plan realistically. Waiting allows them to experience the frustration and joy of anticipation and to understand that life doesn't end when you don't get everything, every time.

Talking about Behavior
Kathy's Q & A

QUESTION

My wife and I are allergic to fur and feathers. We've always known we couldn't have pets but now our three-year-old son, Henry, wants a dog. He just loves to play with the neighbor's dog. How can we explain to him that he can't have a pet? We hate to see him hurt and disappointed and want to give him the news in the easiest way possible.

ANSWER

Give him the news in a matter-of-fact way. Explain to him that you and his mother can't have animals in the house because you have allergies. It's actually very simple. If you let him know that this is just how it is, he may be disappointed but he'll be fine. If you become over-wrought or start your explanation with something like: "I know this is going to be very difficult for you but..." he'll be more upset. Children often look to their parents for signals on how to react to news.

In the meantime, he has the neighbor's pet to play with. If he continues to enjoy animals, there are other ways he can have contact with them. Once he's old enough he can walk dogs for friends and neighbors, or volunteer at the local SPCA.

Plenty of children grow up without pets for a variety of reasons and they turn out just fine.

QUESTION

My school-age children are very susceptible to advertising. We talk about the ads they see and they are clear on how they're being manipulated. But they only understand when it's not something they want. When it is, they'll bug me until I give in. What can I do?

ANSWER

Kids today are big business and the advertising industry is busy wooing their dollars. According to a YTV survey in Canada in 1998, children between the ages of nine and 13 had $1.5 billion of disposable income. In his book, *Allowances, Dollars and Sense*, author Paul W. Lermitte notes that it's not surprising that the advertising heat targeted at children is intensifying.

So what are we to do?

You are already taking the first step. Advertising is there, so we need to teach our children to be wise consumers. Sit down with them and talk about the ads. Compare product ads and their claims. Do your children really think all products can offer everything that they claim? Do they choose their friends according to the runners they wear?

Understand that fitting in is very important, particularly as your children reach their preteen years. And fitting in includes the right clothes and things, like Pokémon cards. There's nothing wrong with allowing them some of the things they need to fit in, but don't become a slave to their fashion desires. The trick is to plan ahead. Let them know before going shopping what it is you are prepared to buy, what choices they can make and the amount of money you've budgeted to spend.

If they want more, there are other options. They can save money to make up the difference between what you think is reasonable and what they want. They can ask for those designer runners for their birthday or Christmas.

Children benefit by having to wait. They need to learn to wait, anticipate, save, wish and to plan for what it is that they want. In some cases they need to make choices, so they learn to set priorities for what it is they want the most. Teaching this to children is not fun and a lot of parents don't have the time or patience. Giving in to children has an immediate short-term payoff for parents. Their children are temporarily quiet and well behaved. It avoids that particular temper tantrum in the mall.

Which leads to your comment that the kids bug you until you give in. Well, you know the answer to that. Don't give in. Don't argue. Practice a one-sentence answer to their request and just repeat it until they get the message. A good example is, "No." Another answer is, "You can save your money to buy that." When they respond, "But that'll take forever and I *need* it now!" your response can be: "You *want* it now. And you can save your money to buy it."

It's important that your children learn the difference between wants and needs. They need school clothes and you will buy the best quality for the most reasonable price. They can choose from among the styles in the determined price range. If they want to upgrade, they can pay the difference.

It's also a good idea to avoid saying you can't afford something. The implication is that if you had the money, you'd buy it. It's better to say that spending that much on runners is not in your budget. That lets them know that you will only spend a reasonable amount of money on any product.

It's also fine to splurge occasionally. The trick is to use the word splurge so they know it's a treat, and to plan ahead so it's not a case of you caving into the nagging.

QUESTION
My toddler has taken to throwing temper tantrums. How can I deal with this?

ANSWER
Tempter tantrums are pretty typical behavior for a toddler. Toddler tantrums are most often the result of frustration. They have a strong belief in themselves as they assert, "I can do it myself!" When they try to do everything they want, they simply can't. So they lose it.

Tantrums can often be prevented. It's a good idea to create an environment that allows children a certain amount of independence and success. Choose clothing that is easy for them to put on, get sturdy stools which permit them to reach the sink to wash their own hands and put toys on low shelves. These will all help your child to feel competent and reduce the frustration. The more he can do for himself, the better he'll feel about himself.

Little ones who are tired or hungry are more likely to overreact. Children who are fed on time and have regular naps are less likely to have tantrums. It's easy for little ones to get overtired and be unable to handle themselves. It's up to us to read the signals and act before there's a problem.

Of course, we can't prevent all tantrums. During the tantrum the best thing you can do is keep an eye on him so he doesn't hurt himself, and let it happen. Don't try to talk to him. He can't hear.

There's a point at which you're likely to see a change in the tantrum. One minute he's raging and the next he's looking scared. Now he needs you, because he isn't sure he can stop. Hold him and reassure him that he's going to be okay and help him settle himself.

With toddlers, once it's over just move on.

Sometimes a tantrum is a way to relieve stress. They may use some little event to blow off some steam. We do the same thing when we find ourselves blowing up over some little thing or crying at a movie.

The trick is to pay attention. When is he most likely to have a tantrum? What can you do to prevent it?

QUESTION

My five-year-old has a tantrum every time I say no. What can I do?

ANSWER

As children age, their tantrums change. Tantrums in older children are more often an attempt to get their own way.

They can, however, be a result of frustration, hunger or being overtired as with the younger children. In those cases, as in the answer above, you can try to prevent them. While these tantrums are a concern and annoying, it's easier to be compassionate.

When a child is throwing a tantrum to get her own way, we often get angry. Then we join in the process. If you watch the interaction between parent and child, sometimes it's difficult to distinguish who exactly is having the tantrum.

Don't take the tantrum personally. She doesn't really hate you, and it's okay that she thinks you're being mean to her. Don't rise to the bait. Try to stay quiet and go on with whatever you're doing.

If she does eventually get her own way, you can count on the fact that she'll try again. It's the job of children to push the limits and it's our job to set and enforce those limits. If you've said no, stick to it.

You may notice that a certain rule always precipitates a reaction, even when you don't back down. It's time to revisit that rule. It may be that it's no longer appropriate. For example, she wants to visit her friend two doors down and wants to go alone. Maybe it's now time to let her go. (You can arrange for the other parent to call you when she arrives.)

Chapter 10

PRIVATE FAMILY MATTERS
WHAT KIDS NEED (AND DON'T NEED) TO KNOW

NINE-YEAR-OLD JULIA CAME INTO THE KITCHEN AND SAID TO HER mom, Carol, "Uncle Harry has fallen asleep at the table again. Why is he always so tired?" It was a family birthday dinner and, as usual, Harry had had too much to drink and quietly passed out at the table. The one saving grace was that he was a nice quiet drunk.

Carol realized she would have to talk to her daughter about this family secret. The next morning at breakfast they had a conversation. Carol explained, "Uncle Harry has a drinking problem, which means that he doesn't know when he's had enough wine."

Julia had many questions: How a drinking problem happens, can't he just stop and why do we invite him anyway? Her mother explained, then Julia said she wanted to call her girlfriend.

Now Carol realized they needed to have a different conversation. There are certain things, she explained to her daughter, that we don't talk about with our friends and neighbors. Uncle Harry's drinking problem is private and Julia needs to keep it private.

Children today know more about adult issues and worries than ever before. Parents in my workshops are expressing concerns about the amount of personal and private information available to our kids.

When I was a child, keeping secrets from children was one of the things parents did. We weren't considered old enough to know. And in many cases this was healthy. Some things were just none of our business.

Why are kids more aware today? The media is one reason. They watch TV and see stories about marital infidelity, workplace harassment and political scandals. When you had to read a newspaper to get this information, kids just missed it.

Also, kids are spending more time around adults. Instead of tearing outside after dinner to play, they are hanging around listening to the very adult after-dinner conversation of their folks. And in some cases they are hearing way too much.

Children do not need to know about sexual problems between their parents or the fact that Grandma likes their sister best. Gossip about neighbors or workplace colleagues is also none of their business. Remember, just because they don't seem to be paying attention doesn't mean that our kids aren't listening. Save private conversations for when you are truly alone.

However, there are some times when children should know the truth.

When a parent or grandparent is sick the children should know what is happening. They are aware of the situation and facts will clarify, not confuse. They know something is wrong but don't know what. Tell them the truth and help them deal with it. The amount of medical information you give a child will depend on her age and how many questions she asks. Also, let her visit. A visit from a grandchild is often a real tonic for a sick grandparent. Of course, you need to control her exuberance and keep it short — an active four-year-old can be exhausting even for a healthy grandparent!

Mental illness is often kept a secret but when a family member is mentally ill it is important that the child understand why Aunt Helen acts so strangely.

WHAT ABOUT MONEY?

Mike drove home in his new car. He'd done his homework — visited a number of dealerships, talked to friends and read the consumer reports — and finally he'd made a choice. He was thrilled. His neighbor, Ken, wandered over to admire the new vehicle. Soon they had the hood up and were engrossed in a conversation about horsepower and engine size. Then Ken asked what he'd paid. Mike muttered something and said he had to go in for dinner. Eight-year-old Ashleigh had been watching the whole thing and followed her dad into the house.

"Daddy, are you mad? You look mad," she asked Mike.

"It's none of his business what I paid. I hate it when people get so personal," he answered.

Money is fraught with minefields when it comes to conversation and privacy. It makes sense to a child that Uncle Harry would be embarrassed if the kids talked about his drinking problem. Money is different. There are degrees of privacy about money and it varies from person to person. You tell eight-year-old Emily that the price of your new house is private, then you turn around and brag to your friend that you got your new coat on sale for just $89.99. Emily knows that she's not to gab about how much money her father makes, but the next day hears a long conversation with the neighbors about the salary scales in the new collective agreement. You need to help your children understand what the rules are in each situation.

In Chapter 11 (Allowances) we'll talk more about children and their own money, but they also need to have a sense of what things cost, what the family can afford and how the family budget works. However, they also need to know that this is private information that stays in the family. By nine or ten years of age most children have a good sense of numbers and money. This is a good time to talk to them about the family finances.

Tell them in round numbers how much money comes into the house each month. Then tell them about all the regular payments, the money that disappears before you can even consider buying shoes or a chocolate bar. It's a great exercise for them. If they need to really see it, take out the Monopoly money and show them where the money goes and how little is left over once the bills are paid. Family finances are private, but all family members deserve to understand them.

When there is a financial downturn, the children may find themselves constantly being snapped at: "Because we can't afford it!" If this is a change then explain it to the children, involve them in the budgeting and let them know it isn't their fault. Reality and reassurance are the watchwords here: There are some financial changes, but Mom and Dad will handle it.

IN OTHER WORDS...

Children are part of the family and whatever is happening will affect them, whether we talk to them about it or not.

Let children know what's happening within the boundaries of their age and ability to understand and give them the opportunity to learn tolerance, acceptance and flexibility when situations change. Protect them from adult-only concerns but inform them when they need to know.

Children learn by watching and as they watch us handle awkward or embarrassing situations they learn how to cope. Julia learned that even though Uncle Harry drinks we still treat him with respect and include him in family events.

Talking about Behavior
Kathy's Q & A

QUESTION

My three-year-old is a generous child and likes to give gifts. This is good; however, she is beginning to want to give away possessions of sentimental value, such as the teddy bear my parents gave her when she was a tiny newborn. It was their first gift to her. On one hand I am proud of her generosity and I'm not sure I should interfere when she decides what to do with her own possessions. On the other hand, some things are too "precious" to give away. What should we do?

ANSWER

You are indeed fortunate to have such a generous child. At her young age many children are just learning to share. However, at this age she is unlikely to understand the ramifications of her generosity.

While it's important that children be permitted to deal with the consequences of their choices, it's our responsibility to moderate these lessons according to their age. At three, she just doesn't understand that giving her stuff away means it's gone forever.

Talk to her about the special possessions and what they mean. Let her know that they are not only important to her but to you and to her grandparents. You might demonstrate by talking about some jewelry you wear not just because you like it but because of what it stands for. A wedding ring is an excellent example.

Make it a rule that she's to talk to you before giving things away. Then you can allow her to present the toy to her friend, but you have helped her make an appropriate choice. You may also have to help her deal with the fact that she has given the toy away forever.

If she has a particular friend she likes to give things to, you could allow her to loan them. In that case make sure you have spoken to the parents so they also understand what is happening.

QUESTION

My 12-year-old daughter used to tell me everything; now, she says very little. I know she keeps a diary. Should I read it to see what she's up to?

ANSWER

Do not read her diary. It's private and personal. Your 12-year-old is absolutely typical. Most children go through this stage. Even those who talk a lot are more likely to discuss neutral topics like sports than their personal lives.

Don't assume she's up to anything. She's simply asserting her independence. She's probably also talking to her friends about more personal things than she did in the past.

If you're worried about her, let her know but don't push her to talk. You can tell her what concerns you. Odds are, however, there's nothing to worry about.

The diaries of young teens are full of hopes and dreams, fantasies and wishes. They rarely document activities. If you read her diary (or her email or go through her purse or backpack) she'll know you don't trust her and she'll be much less likely to ever trust you.

Respect her privacy and let her come to you when she's ready, and this stage will pass more quickly.

QUESTION

My daughter sends a lot of emails to her friends. I read them when she's at school so I can be up to date on what she's thinking and doing. Should I tell her that I'm doing this?

ANSWER

We want to respect our children's privacy. Really we do. But what about email? There it is, right in front of us.

If we just take a peek we'll know what's going on in our children's lives. And that's not like going into their diary or opening envelopes, right? Wrong.

Email often doesn't seem like real mail but it is private correspondence. Not only should you not talk to her about it, you shouldn't read it either!

If you want to build trust with your daughter, you have to actually demonstrate that you trust her. Going into her private email correspondence shows a definite lack of trust.

Besides the very important issue of respect for privacy, which should be reason enough, there are other reasons to stay out of her correspondence. When kids are talking to each other, they are often exaggerating, fantasizing, teasing and just having a great time. If you read her mail out of context, you can get the totally wrong idea. She may also use email to complain about you. She needs and deserves this outlet in private. So stay away.

QUESTION

I have a six-year-old girl who is exploring her body physically. I have heard this is normal and I have tried to explain to her that this is private behavior and she must do it alone in her bedroom or bathroom.

It seems to be very frequent and now is getting to the point where she does not want to wear underpants. Is there anything we can do as parents to steer her away from this activity of hers, or should we just let her keep exploring?

ANSWER

Some children are born more sensual than others and exhibit more interest in their genitals. Others are barely interested. Both are perfectly healthy responses.

You are absolutely correct that she needs to learn that masturbation is a private activity. I applaud you for giving her clear direction without judging her behavior. You may need to repeat this message a number of times. It's important that she learn not to fondle herself in public as this can put her at risk for abuse.

She needs to know what behavior and clothing is appropriate. So wearing underpants when she's out in public is the correct way to behave. Engage her in a conversation about boundaries. Make sure she not only knows that she is to masturbate in private but that no one else is to touch her.

I'd also recommend you pick up the book *More Speaking of Sex*, by Meg Hickling.

Keep talking to your daughter because knowledge leads to good sexual health and protects children from abuse. Abusers look for vulnerable children who don't know about sexual health. They are less likely to tell because they don't have the language.

Chapter 11

ALLOWANCES
HOW MUCH? HOW SOON? FOR WHAT?

TEN-YEAR-OLD DANIEL GETS HIS ALLOWANCE IN CASH EVERY SUNDAY evening. On Monday morning, he decided against the advice of his parents to take all of it to school just so he'd know where it was. When he got home that afternoon, he was devastated. He had lost it all. It fell out of his pocket and he couldn't find it anywhere. He retraced his steps; he reported it to his teacher and the office, but no luck.

On Monday evening Daniel's parents came to a parenting workshop and asked what they should do. Should they replace the lost money? After all, Daniel had looked hard for it and the likelihood is that someone stole it so it wasn't his fault.

What are the goals that Daniel's parents have for their son when he turns 18? If one goal is that he thinks about the consequences of his decisions, how will replacing the money help

Daniel move to this ability? His parents had recommended against taking the money with him and he chose to do so. If his parents replace the lost money are they teaching him to consider the wisdom of his decision?

His parents need to be understanding and sympathetic, and let him cope with the loss. He will not only learn to be more aware of the consequences of his actions; he will learn that his parents have faith in his ability to cope with adversity.

WHAT ABOUT ALLOWANCES?

Money makes the world go round and every child knows that from a very young age.

Children should have some money of their own from about the age of three or four, so that they can learn the value of items they take for granted. They can learn to save and plan ahead (or suffer the consequences of not doing so) and they can know they belong because everyone has some income, no matter how little.

There are different kinds of money. There is the money in bonds or trust accounts for higher education; this doesn't count for young children because they really can't plan that far ahead. There is gift money which is a bonus and fun to receive, and there is some regular discretionary income for each child. This is money she receives simply by being a member of the family and, like food, becomes one of the rights of family membership. This money is the child's to do with as she wishes (within the family rules) so that she can learn from a young age the realities of handling money.

I know what you are thinking. If you just *give* money to your children they will never learn the value of work, they will become selfish and demanding and have unrealistic attitudes.

Well, yesterday I cleaned the toilet, washed the kitchen floor, made my bed, cooked three meals and no one paid me a cent for that work. That work was part of my responsibility of being a member of this family. Each member of the family has certain responsibilities and these responsibilities are tied to their age and ability. These are separate.

As an adult I am paid for work that services those *outside* my family. As a family member I have certain responsibilities and privileges, and one of these privileges is access to a share of the money that comes into the house, access to a share of the food that is bought with that money and access to a share of the leisure activities that are purchased by the family. And that should be true whether I am three or 33.

Children who are paid for work and docked for work undone will grow up believing they should be paid for everything they do. Rather than becoming co-operative members of a family and society, they may always need the answer to the question: "What's in it for me?" Once they are teens and old enough to get part-time work, they may decide they can make better money flipping burgers than doing housework, and "opt out" of work in the home altogether.

While everyone who lives in the house should be expected to do their fair share of the regular chores, there are also opportunities for teens to earn extra money for extra work. One good rule of thumb is, if this is a job you'd hire someone for and if your child is old enough to handle the work, then hire her. Be clear on the rules and expectations for the work. One stumbling block that often arises is timing. Let your teen know when you expect her to do the work and insist that she meet the same deadline you'd expect from anyone else.

Access to money is determined first on the basis of the amount of discretionary money available in the family, then on the realistic needs of the child. Take a look at what your child needs to buy. A preschooler needs just a little money for treats but should have a bank account of her own to help her learn about banking and feel comfortable in a bank.

CLOTHING ALLOWANCES

Teenagers, on the other hand, need more money. If the allowance includes bus passes and clothing the amount needs to be higher than if it is for leisure activities only.

Clothing allowances are wonderful because they remove all the fighting. If your daughter decides to buy the expensive, trendy jeans, she'll discover that she cannot also afford a sweater. You can remain blissfully uninvolved. Kids are ready for a clothing allowance at about 14 and this should be given monthly.

MONEY AND FAMILY PURCHASES

In order to prepare for making more complex purchasing decisions, your children need to learn about spending from you. Take them shopping and talk about your choices. Converse, don't lecture, about the pros and cons of your different options.

Eleven-year-old Gary was fascinated with sports statistics. Where other kids got their sports news from TV, he read the box scores in the newspaper. He lives alone with his father and they were planning on buying a new television set, so Dad gave him the task of doing the research. Gary's interest in numbers and noting how the sports statistics related to the actual game outcome was the perfect background for this job. He checked the Internet for television set reviews, read the sale flyers, phoned stores and after a week came to his dad with a detailed explanation of choices depending on what features they wanted.

He and his dad then took a look at all the information and made their purchase.

Gary learned more about how his dad spends money from that exercise than from hours of lectures, and his father benefited from the research his son had conducted.

TEENS AND JOBS

Part-time work is a real rite of passage for most kids. They earn their own money and, in doing so, they learn to show up on time, work with others, pull their own weight and follow orders.

It starts with babysitting or shoveling walks in the neighborhood. Then it evolves into flipping burgers or working retail. And it can be a positive growing experience.

But it shouldn't be the primary activity for our youngsters. Too many teens are working too many hours. School, family and extracurricular activities as well as some down time must come first. Generally, teens should limit the number of hours they work to 12 per week. That means one after-school shift and one day shift on the weekend is plenty.

Your teen may need you to intercede on his behalf in the workplace. All too often their managers will try to push them to work longer and longer hours. But you need to be clear. Twelve is the limit.

IN OTHER WORDS...

Allowances are the right of every family member within the real limitations of the family income. Household chores are the responsibility of every family member within the real limitations of age, ability and available time. And the two should be seen as separate.

Children in today's society need to learn about money. No matter what your future goals are for your children, they will need to learn how to spend and how to save — and it's far easier to learn it throughout childhood than have it suddenly thrust on you at age 18.

Talking about Behavior
Kathy's Q & A

QUESTION

My 13-year-old has started babysitting for a few neighbors. As a result, she doesn't want to stay home with her younger siblings, who are seven and nine, unless we pay her. Should she be paid for looking after her sister and brother?

ANSWER

Being the oldest child in a family carries both privileges and responsibilities. While most oldest children enjoy the rights to stay up later and go farther afield, they're not as pleased with the extra tasks and expectations commensurate with their age. Generally, every member of the family should be expected to participate in the work of the family without pay and for an oldest this includes a certain amount of babysitting.

But once kids are old enough to make money either by babysitting or taking on part-time jobs, they have difficulty understanding why they should work at home for free when they can get paid outside the home.

One compromise many families have found effective is to pay their child if she has to turn down a paying job to stay home with her siblings. Another approach is to negotiate with her the amount of free babysitting you feel is appropriate. If, for example, you have a regular activity requiring babysitting one evening a week, you might ask her to be available that evening and one weekend night a month.

It is important that you discuss this with her. She needs to know that while you don't believe that she should be paid every time she babysits her siblings, there is some room for negotiation. The goal is to respect her desire and ability to make extra money while still expecting that she will contribute to the family by staying home with her young siblings simply because she's needed.

QUESTION

My ten-year-old son wants to play computer games constantly. When I suggest he do something else he looks at me like I'm crazy and says there's nothing else he wants to do. What can I do?

ANSWER

First look at how much time your son is actually spending at the computer and what the impact is on the rest of his life. Does he have friends? How is he doing in school?

If he's doing fine then it's simply a matter of deciding how much time you think is appropriate for him to be on the computer playing games. Sit down with him and let him know that from now on he can play games for, let's say, an hour a day, after he has completed his homework. You can say, "When you finish your homework, you may have one hour of computer game time." Don't expect him to be happy with this decision. It's not your job to make him happy. It's your job to help him have some balance in his activities.

If you realize that the computer has become his whole life, you will want to talk to him and let him know that his schoolwork comes first and that he needs to keep his marks up in order to have computer time. You may also need to encourage him to join in some extracurricular activity so that he can connect with other youngsters of his age who share his interests. If there's a computer club at the school or community center, this is a great way to help him make friends. He gets to play on his beloved computer but in a social setting.

Some children have trouble settling to sleep after playing games. So you may also want to have the computer turned off a half-hour before bedtime. This means that if he procrastinates with homework, there may not be an hour left. Make sure you give him a warning before the computer needs to be turned off so he can arrange to save his game at the appropriate point. If you just pull the plug he may lose all the progress he's gained and that's just not fair.

Take a look at the games he's playing. Replace violent games with creative ones. Have him teach you how to play so you are aware of what he's doing. Children love to teach their parents and in most cases are more adept at all aspects of computer use than adults.

You can also be flexible with the rules when he has friends over or on weekends.

QUESTION

I have three children. One is two years old, one is four and the third is seven. I have just started a new job that will require a number of business trips. How can I best prepare the children for these trips?

ANSWER

Preparing kids for out-of-town trips varies according to the age of the child.

For your toddler it's best to wait until the day before the trip to announce your imminent departure. Be matter-of-fact but make sure you do tell him. At dinnertime you might just say, "Tomorrow I'll be having dinner at a hotel in Denver. Denver is pretty far away so I won't be able to see you but I will phone."

That way when he asks about you the next day, Daddy can remind him by saying, "Remember, Mommy said she was going to be in Denver, but she's going to phone in ten minutes."

Call at the same time every day. Your toddler may not want to talk to you but he will know that you haven't forgotten him.

When you get home he may ignore you for a while. If that happens help him to express his anger or hurt: "You don't like it when Mommy goes away." Then just listen or watch his reactions. You can reassure him, "It's okay to be upset."

With her developing sense of time and need to understand what's going to happen, your preschooler needs more notice than a toddler. You can tell her a week or so before you leave to give her time to get used to the idea that you'll be away.

Call home at the same time every day and tell her little details about your trip. She'll love to know that your hotel blanket is blue and that you had cut-up fruit for breakfast. That way she can imagine what's happening in your life and may reciprocate with some details of her day. Tape yourself reading her favorite bedtime stories so she can listen to you tell a story as she falls asleep.

When you get home she may be either extra clingy or slightly rebellious. Give her the attention she needs and let her talk about how she feels about you traveling, but don't permit outright misbehavior. She needs to learn how to handle anger or disappointment in an appropriate way.

Your seven-year old can have even more notice. You can let him know as soon as you do. Then let him participate in planning his activities while you're away. Is he going to need a ride to soccer practice?

Just like with the younger kids, stay in touch while you're away. But sit down with him and talk about when would be the best time for you to call. When you do phone, talk to him about specific topics. If you ask, "How are things?" the likely response will be: "Oh, okay, I guess." But a question like: "How did the project you were working on turn out? Did the teacher like it?" allows him to focus and start a conversation.

He's likely to be totally matter-of-fact when you come home, so don't expect a big fuss. If he's interested tell him about the trip, but otherwise just get on with your regular routine.

All the kids will like to get a souvenir from the trip, but they don't need big gifts. A postcard with a picture of the hotel or a little soap is enough to say, "I was thinking of you." You could start a ritual of bringing home a place mat with a local photo. These are inexpensive and easy to find, and will build up a collection of reminders of all your trips.

QUESTION

I want my two-year-old to be a good reader. What can I do?

ANSWER

Read to him. Children love to hear stories and when you read to him regularly he'll learn to love the printed word.

Every time he shows an interest in anything, find a book or article and read that to him. If you tie his interests into reading he'll learn that books are a source of valuable information.

Most libraries have story times for little ones. Take him there so that the library becomes a comfortable place. He'll get used to being there. Take books out of the library. Let him choose some and you choose some.

There are some great magazines for children. The next time one of his relatives asks what to get him for a gift, suggest a subscription. I used to do this for my nieces and nephews. I loved the fact that my gift came into their homes across the country each month. They loved the fact that they got these cool magazines.

You can also make books part of the normal gift-giving routine. I got books for Christmas and my birthday all through my childhood. I loved it. I also remember seeing my parents read. Modeling behavior is the best teaching tool we have. If your son sees you reading for pleasure, he'll learn to do the same.

Introduce children to poetry. For youngsters there are wonderful books of nonsense rhymes and simple verses. But don't limit all their exposure to children's books. In many families there is a ritual of reading *A Christmas Carol* each year by reading a chapter a night. Others find that reading a more advanced book during summer holidays is fun.

You are now reading this book. Is your child watching?

Chapter 12

PUTTING IT ALL TOGETHER
THE FAMILY MEETING

IT'S TUESDAY NIGHT IN THE MOORE HOUSE. TYPICAL OF MANY
families today, the evening schedule is a nightmare. Fourteen-
year-old Stacey needs a ride to her band practice at seven o'clock.
Eleven-year-old Jonah has to be at the community center for his
swimming practice that also starts at seven — and he too needs a
ride. The band practice and the swimming pool are nowhere near
each other. George, their father, has an important client dinner
and won't be home until about nine.

It's now 6:45 p.m. The kids and Elizabeth, their mom, have
finished eating and no one is in a panic. How is this possible?
Shouldn't Jonah be racing around trying to find his swim gear,
both kids yelling at Mom that they need a ride right now and
Mom tearing her hair out trying to figure out a way to drive in
two directions at once?

The Moores have a plan. Last Sunday after brunch the family sat down together, as they do every week, and had a family meeting. In the planning section of this meeting the Tuesday night dilemma came to light and the family moved into problem-solving mode. Jonah recalled that last week his friend Tommy had come with them so he called Tommy and arranged a ride with his family. Simple solution, right?

For many families the problem isn't finding a simple solution, it's thinking ahead far enough to make it happen. Life today is too complex to leave the planning to the last minute. The way to make planning ahead a reality is family meetings.

For many of us, family meetings are the stuff of television sitcoms. A problem develops in the home of the TV family and a parent, usually Dad, yells "We need a family meeting!" So the concept of the family meeting becomes associated with a problem and probably means a lecture at best, a punishment at worst. Who needs it?

Television has it all wrong. Family meetings are a regularly scheduled coming together of all the family members to plan the weekly schedule, to assign chores, to distribute allowances, to handle disputes and to celebrate achievements.

Family Meetings that Work

Use the following ideas to keep your family meetings on track:

• **HAVE A REGULAR TIME AND PLACE**

When meetings are held only because there is a problem, adults and children alike will grow to hate them. When meetings are held at regular, scheduled intervals there is nothing to dread.

With regular meetings, problems are often raised before they become a major source of conflict. Also, once a schedule is accepted, the family will find it easier to plan to attend.

• **INVITE ALL FAMILY MEMBERS TO PARTICIPATE**

This includes any live-in members of the extended family and young children. Participation isn't mandatory; however, as decisions made affect the whole family, attendance is a good idea.

• MAKE ALL PARTICIPANTS EQUAL

This does not mean voting. It does mean that all members have equal opportunity to introduce topics and to speak. Decisions are reached by consensus.

If there is no option (a non-negotiable family rule) children can express their opinions but must know that this is a non-negotiable item.

• ROTATE THE CHAIRMANSHIP

Children not only enjoy having a turn to chair; they will also learn about meeting procedures and rules.

• BUILD AN AGENDA

An agenda will keep you on track and organized (remember organization is one of the goals of this activity!).

• TAKE MINUTES

A written record of decisions solves disputes and permits a follow-up evaluation.

• HAVE A FOLLOW-UP TIME FOR EVALUATION

It is very important for everyone to know exactly when a decision can be re-evaluated and changed if necessary.

• FINALLY

Family meetings are not a time for parents to dump on the children! Have fun, lighten up and enjoy the time together as a family.

Six Steps to Solving a Problem

When a conflict exists, this process helps participants work together toward a solution:

1. IDENTIFY AND DEFINE THE CONFLICT

Take as much time as necessary to listen until a clear definition of the problem is presented.

2. GENERATE SOLUTIONS

Ask children for their ideas. Accept all ideas, don't evaluate, judge or belittle, and keep allowing possible solutions until there are no more ideas.

3. EVALUATE

Everyone has an opportunity to state their feelings about the list of ideas created in the previous step.

4. DECIDE ON THE BEST SOLUTION

After the evaluation, one solution usually emerges as ideal. If not, use consensus to select one, or create a solution from a combination of ideas.

5. IMPLEMENT

This is the step that is most often missed and causes problems. Once the solution is selected, make a note of what is needed to make it happen. Who will do what, and when?

6. FOLLOW-UP EVALUATION

Set a time for a follow-up evaluation to see how well your solution is working; the next scheduled meeting is usually the best idea.

There are some unexpected advantages to family meetings. Twenty years from now you'll have the minutes of all the meetings you held while your children were growing up. You'll be able to relive the true day-to-day realities of their childhood. It's better than a photo album.

Your children will learn how to handle meetings and how to problem-solve. Whether it's how to handle the need for rides to events or a dispute between the kids about choosing television programs, problem-solving is an important component of family meetings — and life!

Once your kids know that you'll actually listen to their ideas and work with them to develop a solution, they will participate with energy and creativity. Make sure, though, that you let them know the bottom line. When you start to work through a problem, it's important for them to remember that there are family rules, which will be honored, and that there are limits to what you can and will do. In other words, you won't quit your job to make certain that you're always available when they want you, and you won't send little sister off to Grandma's for the rest of her life to prevent her getting into her brother's stuff.

IN OTHER WORDS...

Family meetings not only solve problems and smooth the family's daily activities, they also teach your kids how to work together, how to respect the needs of others and how to develop solutions that are appropriate and successful. This process is great because you see immediate benefits, while at the same time you're raising kids of good character.

Talking about Behavior
Kathy's Q & A

QUESTION

I have two children, aged five and eight. They love to get involved in projects that drag on for days. A few weeks ago they built a town complete with tents created from blankets and sleeping bags. They involved all their stuffed animals and dolls. The family room was taken over and they wanted to leave the mess in place for days. Now they want to paint and leave the sheets drying all over the place. How can I get them to keep their space clean?

ANSWER

The first question is, why? These activities are healthy, creative and fun. I'd encourage you to let them use the family room for their ongoing projects. They can clean the room when the game is over tomorrow or next week.

When we expect kids to keep their play spaces clean and tidy we stifle their creativity. Any creative process makes what we often call a mess but can really represent positive activity. Think about what the kitchen looks like in the middle of a jam-making session or the bedroom when you've decided to paint.

You can have some reasonable rules. For example, you may insist that any food garbage be cleared away before bed every evening as that can cause a smell and attract unwelcome little animals. Or, if you have a social event coming up, you can ask them to have the room clean for that day.

Kids need a space they can use. Whether it's a corner in the living room, their bedrooms or a family room, they flourish when they can develop imaginative games over time.

You can also get into the spirit of the game by bringing them a picnic lunch and joining them on the floor for a feast of sandwiches and juice or by letting them camp out in their tent rather than having to sleep in their beds.

This kind of play is also inexpensive. They can incorporate their existing toys into the process, use old blankets and pillows and you can donate your old clothing and jewelry (as long they're old enough to know not to try to eat it) for dress-up.

QUESTION

Whenever we say no to my eight-year-old daughter she goes to the other parent to get the answer she wants. My husband and I feel like we're in the middle of a tug-of-war. What can we do?

ANSWER

A tug-of-war only works when everyone plays. If one side refuses to pull, the game is over.

As much as possible, set house rules together, so, when she comes with a request, you're both likely to have the same response. Family meetings, where rules are discussed and set with all family members present, are a good idea. Then when she comes to a parent with a request to do something normally not permitted you can simply say, "Do you remember the rule about that?"

If she comes to her dad with a request he's not sure about, he can respond with, "What did your mother say?" Then he can suggest that he'll talk to Mom and get back to the child later. (Don't keep her waiting too long.) Once you start doing this, she'll stop the game.

QUESTION

My nine-year-old daughter, Sally, dawdles when she does her chores. She never finishes the few things we ask her to do but still wants to go out with her friends. I generally let her go because I don't want her to miss the social aspect of friendship. She promises to do her chores later but it never happens. What should I do?

ANSWER

First, it helps if chores are part of a discussion at family meetings and the children get to make some choices. Not doing any chores is not an acceptable choice, but whether to vacuum the living room or clean the bathroom is. Another part of the rule is no going out until chores are done.

Let's say it's Sally's job to vacuum the living room on Saturday. And it's Saturday and the living room is not clean. Sally's been up for hours and has been a busy little beaver. She's watched a TV show, surfed the Internet and sent some emails, and each time you mention the living room she's gone to the bathroom. Can't stop her from doing that, can you?

Now her friend has called and said she has free movie tickets and her mom is going to drive them to the theater. What a great deal. But, what about the vacuuming? She'll do it later, she says.

Nope. She knows that she has a responsibility at home. She can go to the movies when she finishes her work. Now here's the trick. Don't get sucked into all the arguments. Just remind her that she has this responsibility and must do her vacuuming. You don't need to point out how much time she's wasted, just that she has a job to do.

And if she misses the movie you can be sympathetic — but that's all.

QUESTION

I love to take my two-year-old daughter Adriana for walks. But she can drag a five-minute walk to the corner into half an hour as she explores everything in sight. How can I get her moving?

ANSWER

The only way to get her moving is to put her in a stroller. When adults go for a walk they are looking for exercise and movement. But for your two-year-old, it's a voyage of discovery.

I remember the time my neighbor took his 19-month-old twins for a walk. The children were in the lead, and in no hurry whatsoever. A rock grabbed the attention of one and the other decided that swinging our gate back and forth was the order of the day. Dad stood patiently by, responding to the activities of the children. Eventually they moved on and walked about ten yards, until a bug caught their attention — so they squatted on the sidewalk watching. They got about halfway up the block and turned around. Dad watched as the children explored driveways and cracks in the sidewalk. They didn't get far, but they sure had a great time.

The trick is to relax and enjoy your daughter's pace. You'll see the neighborhood through new eyes. The goal is to get some fresh air and spend some child-centered time with Adriana.

If you do need to get somewhere you can make it a game. Have a race, point out something up the block, swing her up in your arms and take some giant steps.

Chapter 13

CHILD OF THE COMMUNITY
THE WORLD BEYOND THE FAMILY

WHEN 12-YEAR-OLD MATTHEW WALKS INTO THE CORNER GROCERY
store, the owner greets him by name. Up and down the street
Matthew can say hello to his neighbors. This isn't a mystical television town or a tiny village. He lives in a residential neighborhood in a large city.

But since he was young, Matthew's parents have introduced
Matt to his neighborhood. They took him to the corner store and
introduced him to the owner. He and his parents walk a lot and
talk about what they see, about what to avoid, about where the
Block Parents live and their role in his young life. They have
traced the safest routes to and from school, his friends' homes
and the park. Now that he is older, his parents have taken him on
public transit. They're teaching him how to be both independent
and safe.

They are also showing him how to become involved in his community. His mother is active in local politics and his father is the chair of the school parent committee.

BUILDING CONNECTIONS

In Chapter 7 ("I Like Me!") we noted that no man is an island. We need to teach our children that they are part of something bigger than themselves and to participate in the larger culture. That might include the family, the classroom or the community.

Fourteen-year-old Lorne plays saxophone in a marching band. The band practices on a field just down the street from his house. Every Saturday afternoon the band members can be seen out marching around the field getting ready for the next community event. They are called upon for store openings and any community parades, so all the band members are connected to the neighborhood.

There are any number of ways kids can become an integral part of where they live: participating in bottle drives to raise money for the school, joining the local Scout troop or playing on a soccer team.

Through these activities they become aware of the world beyond their home and classroom. This awareness is the start of creating an involved citizen of the community.

GIFT GIVING

Gift giving is part of our social rituals. To help our children learn to think about others, to see the world through the eyes of others, we can involve them in the gift-giving rituals. The family is the first and most fundamental culture our children experience. When they learn to give and receive within this environment, they can more easily make the transition to being part of the larger community.

VOLUNTEERISM: GIVING BACK

Matthew's parents are very much an active part of their community so it's no surprise that Matthew is involved with a group of students cleaning up the schoolyard. While family is the first group children experience, school is usually the second. Children of good character may find themselves helping with the recycling program or serving as junior crossing guards. It's the start of community involvement outside the family.

Children can be extremely idealistic and get involved in many different causes. Today we see increasing numbers of youngsters involved in environmental concerns. Support your children in these endeavors. And let them understand that what they're doing is voluntary and now they are part of the volunteer sector.

Volunteering helps our children to think of others (flora, fauna or human) and see themselves as part of a society with some responsibility to their neighborhood or country. Unfortunately, many parents of teens are supporting volunteerism simply because it will look good on their children's résumés or they may make business contacts. It is true, this does happen — but I would hate to think that this is the primary reason for volunteering. Volunteering is about giving something back to the community, helping those in need, and fighting for socially responsible ideas and ideals.

We also need to let our children know about our own volunteer activities. Too often when asked we say we're going to a meeting. Which is true, but it sounds like work. Instead talk about the meeting. Is it a political rally, a non-profit board meeting or a neighborhood watch problem-solving session? Use the word

Volunteer Opportunities for Children

- Help an elderly neighbor by shoveling the walk or raking leaves
- Visit a seniors' home and play games or listen to their stories
- Accompany an elderly neighbor or parent with young kids to help with grocery shopping
- Volunteer at the SPCA
- Join the executive of your sports team
- Clean house or babysit for a neighbor or relative who just had surgery
- Run errands for a sick friend

volunteer. Explain your involvement in a matter-of-fact way and when there are ways your child can participate, bring him along.

CIVIC RESPONSIBILITY

Vote. Vote at all levels and let your children know you vote. Discuss the elections, the issues and the candidates. Explain to your children that when we live in democracy, we all have a responsibility to help choose our representatives and leaders.

If you work on political campaigns, let the children join you if they wish.

As your children enter their teens they are likely to want to argue politics. Let them. Enjoy the debate. Participate, but don't put your children down — or let them put you down. Demonstrate by your behavior that we all have a right to our opinions.

IN OTHER WORDS...

Our children live in our community, which gives them soccer coaches, friendly storeowners, neighbor friends, babysitters and schools. From the moment they step outside the house, they are in the community, and the more we help them to become connected to and responsible to the community the more we are giving them the gift of being a citizen of good character.

Talking about Behavior
Kathy's Q & A

QUESTION

Our nine-year-old son and his buddies love to gather for roller hockey in the schoolyard, just at the end of our street. I think they're okay to play there by themselves for half an hour or an hour. My husband disagrees; however, he's not willing to go and watch them. This causes a lot of tension and takes the fun out of the whole thing. What to do?

ANSWER

I hate to find myself in the middle of a couple argument but I'm with you.

A group of nine-year-olds should be perfectly fine playing together without adult supervision. As a matter of fact, it's healthier for them to be playing a pick-up game on their own.

Children today are being overprotected and denied the opportunities to work things out with their friends on their own. They need to be able to walk to school, play in the park or go to the corner store without us constantly hovering.

The problem is that we are so nervous about their safety. In fact, it's not as dangerous as it seems but media coverage of stories in which children are hurt or abducted are so pervasive and frightening we lose our perspective. The trick is to make sure that your children are not alone, that they're playing and walking in groups. You can also increase their safety by having them meet the neighbors, including local storeowners.

We need to figure out ways to allow our children to take back the parks and start to play outside again.

QUESTION

We live in a very homogenous community and I want my children to appreciate cultural diversity. How can I best do that?

ANSWER

We want our children to appreciate the diversity we offer in our society. We certainly want them to be tolerant and not display any signs of racism or prejudice.

Like so many things we teach our children, it's mainly about us. We are the role models. So it's important to be clear on your own feelings before you attempt to deal with your kids. They can see through you when you say one thing and do another.

Then it all starts when they're little. When your children are toddlers and preschoolers, make sure that their toys and books reflect the diversity of the community. When they simply see it all around them, inclusivity becomes part of their lives.

In early elementary school, start talking to them about diversity when the occasion arises. They may not really appreciate what you're saying but it will prepare them to hear it as they mature.

Teach them about their own heritage, too. Let them know that we all have roots. They can have a sense of pride in their background and then appreciate how others feel.

When they're confronted with examples of prejudice, talk to them. Explain the history of racism and let them know that for your family it's unacceptable.

QUESTION

My children attend a school five blocks away from our home. Should I let them walk to school?

ANSWER

Absolutely, once children are old enough for elementary school they are old enough to walk five blocks. You need to start preparing for the walk in August. I know that seems a little early but they need to learn how to get themselves to and from school. For most of our kids that means they need to learn the walking route.

Walking to school is an important part of their education. Yes, school is about reading, 'riting and 'rithmetic. But it's also about growing up and becoming more independent. The walk allows them to leave the safety and security of home and make their way to school. The walk also gives them some exercise. That makes it easier for them to sit still in class, to pay attention and learn. Teachers prefer to have kids walk in the morning so they are prepared to settle down until recess.

So let's go. Step one is to walk to school with the kids. Have a running commentary on where you are, what to watch out for and point out the Block Parent homes. Then have them take you on the walk. They take the lead, they do the talking. Soon, they are walking ahead, with you simply following.

By the first day of school they will be pros. Of course you'll worry — what parent doesn't? — but you'll be able to trust that they can do it.

Go to the Parent Committee meeting and talk about the importance of children walking to school and encourage all the parents to have their kids walking. Soon the sidewalks will be filled with students so none will be alone. The bigger kids will keep an eye on the younger ones.

If there are busy streets suggest that there be crossing guards at those intersections to help the children make their way safely and independently to school.

There are some situations when the streets are simply too dangerous to cross or there are no other kids coming from the same direction as yours. In this case, remember the goal is to help our children learn how to get themselves to school, how to become safe pedestrians and get some exercise.

So make accommodations to suit the situation. One parent I spoke to told me that her kids had to cross a highway with no traffic lights or crossing guards. So she walked them across the busy street and let them finish the walk for the last two blocks, and met them at the same intersection after school. Some parent groups have created "walking school busses," in which parents take turns walking the route to school, picking up kids on the way until the children learn how to walk together and eventually can handle it on their own.

QUESTION

We're moving from Toronto to Calgary next month. I want to make the move as comfortable as possible for my children. What can I do to ease the transition?

ANSWER

Moving is hard work, even without considering children. Most parents wish they could somehow put their children on hold as they try to keep the house perfectly clean to be sold and as they organize, sort and pack the accumulated paraphernalia of their life in the current house.

But what about the children? You're already on the right track. It's hard to be aware of their concerns in the hurly-burly of selling and making all the necessary arrangements. But they do have concerns.

While the decision to move must be made by the adults, the children can be involved in a discussion about the reasons for the decision. You can make moving a creative adventure for children rather than a trauma. As a bonus, some of this positive and creative energy will pass on to you.

There are some tips parents can remember when they are moving:

• Explain to the children what's going to happen. They'll want all the details, such as where they're going to sleep, whether they can bring their toys and whether Calgary has a McDonalds.

• Involve them in preparing the house to be shown and encourage the realtor to recognize their help.

• Arrange a going-away party for them. They need to say good-bye to their friends in a structured way. Make sure you have the addresses (including email) of their closest friends so they can keep in touch if they wish.

• If you're going to choose your new house after you get to Calgary, take them to see it once you have made an offer. This allows them to get excited about their new home right from the start. If you have two or three houses you are seriously considering, allow older children to see them and participate in the discussion of which to choose.

• Once you have bought a new house, involve the children in choosing their bedrooms, decorations, furniture or whatever choices directly involve them. Also include them in the decisions about the main living areas of the house (within choices you can handle).

• Have children help with the packing. On moving day, younger children should be elsewhere with friends or a sitter. Older children can be helping.

It's easier for the kids to make new friends when they attend school. You may be concerned about having your kids change school mid-year. But in fact it often works out better. When your kids are the only new ones, the teachers can really focus on helping them get settled into the new school. Joining the local soccer team or scout troop will help them make friends and enjoy themselves.

If you do have to move in the summer, it may be very difficult for your kids to meet other children. Help them discover what activities attract the kids in your new neighborhood. The local community center or libraries are good places to start. Is there a day camp or swimming lessons that they can join right away? Head over to the local park. Often there is a youth worker or park attendant arranging activities for the kids. Talk to your new neighbors or ask co-workers about summer activities for kids. You may find that a colleague right down the hall has a youngster who can introduce your daughter to the neighborhood.

CONCLUSION

WHO IS IN CHARGE ANYWAY? WHEN I WAS GROWING UP IN THE '50s the rules were clear:

"Obey all adults."

"Because I said so, that's why!"

"It's disrespectful to ever question authority."

"I don't care what she said to you, she's older than you so you just be polite and say nothing."

Children were to unquestionably obey all adults and not question any requests.

In the '60s we started to understand that in order to stay safe, sometimes children need to say no. We learned that when we can help children understand the reasons for the rules and limitations placed on them, they become analytical adults. And we began to believe that children have a right to their own voice and deserve to be listened to.

But, as I've demonstrated throughout this book, in some cases we've gone too far. There's a big difference between saying no as a matter of course and saying no when it matters. There are also developmental considerations. No two-year-old is going to happily accept the reasons why sometimes they need to walk, not run or speak quietly. They just need to do it.

Parents are in charge. Our job is to set the standard for our children's behavior. We do that by clarifying our values so we have a touchstone for parenting decisions. We develop routines that work, watch our own behavior so that we are living the way we want our kids to live and we use positive discipline strategies. We help our children to become valuable members of their community through community activities and volunteerism. We make decisions at family meetings where all opinions can be voiced, but the children know that only some decisions are negotiable. In doing this, we help our children to develop high self-esteem and become valued members of their community.

THE OUTCOME

The fog rolled in, enveloping John and me in a magical world. Our home overlooks the working port of Vancouver and we are classic empty-nesters since our children moved on a number of years ago. We were sitting on our front balcony, listening to the foghorns blare over the water. And we talked.

Our children are in their 30s now, and we were remembering when we sat on the foggy beach on the west coast of Vancouver Island, over three decades ago, and set goals for ourselves as parents and for our children.

It's been quite a ride, with a full complement of adventures as our children grew through infancy, childhood, the teen years, university and into careers. As they were growing up we bandaged a lot of scrapes and bruises and helped them through life's disappointments. Thankfully they were spared serious illness, injury and trauma. Now our daughter, Chelsea, is a geotechnical engineer and our son, Foley, is the production manager in his father's communications company. They both live nearby in Vancouver and we remain a very close family.

Parenting is not a lottery. Having children who grow up to be well-adjusted, self-disciplined adults takes diligent, consistent, conscientious parenting by hard-working moms and dads. When I see kids who grew up straight, I give full credit to their parents. When I see young adults who just don't seem to reach adult maturity, I wonder if they received as much help and firm guidance as they needed during their formative years.

It's not always easy. Some children are definitely easier to raise than others. Parents who have children with health or

behavior problems face tough challenges. Unemployment, parent illness, divorce or bereavement are amongst a few of the extra burdens that some parents carry. Whatever our situation — or theirs — our kids need us to do our very best to rise to the challenge of raising well-adjusted young men and women.

The goal-setting my husband and I did so many years ago helped us with the challenging job called parenting. I think back to that day and know that the journey has been worth every sleepless night, every worrying illness, every misbehaving child who needed my direction and all the times when I wondered whether I was doing the right thing with my kids.

I am now the parent of two adults I am proud to call friends. They remind me every day, with their integrity, their caring for others, their wisdom and their love that this parenting job is worth a thousand other tasks. When I asked them what they thought of this book, they simply said, "Well, that's how we were raised, so there were no surprises."

All parents who look back on their child-raising years recognize that it was hard work. But like all challenging jobs, the rewards are plentiful. For me, the joys of child-raising have always outweighed the difficulties.

Your children are fortunate, because you have just finished reading a parenting book. This means you are thoughtful about the parenting job you're doing and you're interested enough to want to learn more.

Four important considerations in successful parenting are setting goals, learning as much as you can about child-raising, having a discipline plan and developing positive communications skills. But the most important factor is your relationship with each of your children, and your knowledge of what makes that child tick.

Nobody knows my children better than their dad and I do, and nobody knows your children better than you. Trust yourself, and realize that you are the best parent for your children.

Mental illness
   Of family member 115
Misbehavior 42, 44–46, 65
   Prevention of 44
Modeling
   Imitating 32–34, 36
Modesty 34–35
Money 115–16, 120
More Speaking of Sex 119
Moving to a new place 145–47

N
Neighborhood
   Introducing child 139
   Walking to school 144–45

P
Parent involvement
   In school 82–83, 144–45
Parent leadership 17
Parenting education 11, 50
Parenting Today 11
Places of worship 95–96
Planning ahead 43–44, 88,
   94, 96, 132
Power struggles 46–48
Praise 75, 76, 77
Preschool
   Co-operative preschools
   82–83
Preschooler
   Independence 58–59
   Manners 87
   Routine 27
   Staying in bed 71–72
   Stepchild 50–56

Prevention
   Of misbehavior 44
Problem-solving 133–34
Punishment
   Versus discipline 42–43

Q
Quality time 66–67

R
Reading
   To child 71, 129
   Model reading 129
Respect 35, 117–18
Restaurant
   With children 94, 96–97
Rewards 81–82
Role models 17–18, 32–33,
   36, 143–44
Role of parents
   As leaders 17
Rules 149

S
School
   First week 28–29
   Homework 37–38
   Parent involvement 83,
   144–45
Self-esteem 75–81
Setting the standards 17,
   48
Shyness 89
Social order 80
Spanking 42–43

ABOUT THE AUTHOR

An acclaimed speaker on the tough job of parenting, Kathy Lynn has developed and conducted thousands of education sessions for parents and professionals over her 25-year career. She is a Certified Canadian Family Educator, and serves as the parenting education advisor to the Council of Parent Participation Preschools in British Columbia.

Kathy is the host and executive producer of the weekly open-line radio program *Parenting Today*. She also writes a column on parenting issues for *Today's Parent* magazine. She has recorded three of her most popular workshops, "Discipline ... Steps to Success," "Stop It You Two!" and "I Like Me."